BESS WALLACE TRUMAN

MODERN FIRST LADIES

Lewis L. Gould, Editor

TITLES IN THE SERIES

Helen Taft: Our Musical First Lady, Lewis L. Gould

Ellen and Edith: Woodrow Wilson's First Ladies, Kristie Miller

First Lady Florence Harding: Behind the Tragedy and Controversy, Katherine A. S. Sibley

Grace Coolidge: The People's Lady in Silent Cal's White House, Robert H. Ferrell

Lou Henry Hoover: Activist First Lady, Nancy Beck Young

Eleanor Roosevelt: Transformative First Lady, Maurine Beasley

Mamie Doud Eisenhower: The General's First Lady, Marilyn Irvin Holt

Jacqueline Kennedy: First Lady of the New Frontier, Barbara A. Perry

Lady Bird Johnson: Our Environmental First Lady, Lewis L. Gould

Betty Ford: Candor and Courage in the White House, John Robert Greene

Rosalynn Carter: Equal Partner in the White House, Scott Kaufman

Nancy Reagan: On the White House Stage, James G. Benze Jr.

Barbara Bush: Presidential Matriarch, Myra G. Gutin

Hillary Rodham Clinton: Polarizing First Lady, Gil Troy

BESS WALLACE TRUMAN

HARRY'S WHITE HOUSE "BOSS"

SARA L. SALE

UNIVERSITY PRESS OF KANSAS

Published by the University Press of Kansas (Lawrence, Kansas 66045), which was organized by the Kansas Board of Regents and is operated and funded by Emporia State University, Fort Hays State University, Kansas State University, Pittsburg State University, the University of Kansas, and Wichita State University

Library of Congress Cataloging-in-Publication Data

Sale, Sara L.
Bess Wallace Truman : Harry's White House boss / Sara L. Sale.
p. cm. — (Modern first ladies)
Includes bibliographical references and index.
ISBN 978-0-7006-1741-8 (cloth : acid-free paper)
1. Truman, Bess Wallace. 2. Truman, Harry S., 1884–1972—Family. 3. Presidents' spouses—United States—Biography. 4. Presidents—United States—Biography. I. Title.
E814.1.T68S25 2010
978.918092—dc22
[B]
2010021261

British Library Cataloguing-in-Publication Data is available.

Printed in the United States of America
10 9 8 7 6 5 4 3 2 1

The paper used in this publication is recycled and contains 30 percent postconsumer waste. It is acid free and meets the minimum requirements of the American National Standard for Permanence of Paper for Printed Library Materials Z39.48–1992.

In loving memory of my mother,

Margaret Lee Sale

CONTENTS

EDITOR'S PREFACE

When she is remembered at all, Bess Wallace Truman conjures up a series of stereotypes. She was the first lady who gave few interviews, took no positions on major issues, and contented herself with keeping her hat on straight while Harry Truman gave a fiery speech. Coming after the controversial and charismatic Eleanor Roosevelt, she has joined Mamie Eisenhower as a kind of bipartisan lull in the institution of the first lady before the celebrity of Jacqueline Kennedy during the early 1960s. Mrs. Truman destroyed many of her personal letters, and the ones that remain reveal her character only in an occasional moment of candor and insight.

Faced with these obstacles to understanding the complexity of Bess Truman in real life, Sara Sale has penetrated beneath the facade to disclose a woman of influence on her husband's presidency. Harry Truman called her "the Boss," and he attested to her impact on his career in the White House. The Trumans were a working partnership in the presidency from 1945 to 1953, and Sale recaptures how they interacted with post–World War II America to create an administration of historical importance.

Sale is effective in demonstrating the range of Mrs. Truman's interests in charitable events, her involvement in the renovation and reconstruction of the White House, and her symbolic role, along with her daughter, Margaret, in the successful presidential upset victory against Thomas E. Dewey in 1948. The book that Sale has crafted will restore Bess Truman to the position she held at the time her husband was in office. She was indeed a crucial participant in the way he operated as president, and she deserves to share in the historical credit that he has achieved during the past six decades. Above all, Sale brings to her readers a feisty, intelligent first lady who had her head on as straight as her hats.

—Lewis L. Gould

ACKNOWLEDGMENTS

There are a number of people to whom I owe a debt of gratitude. The staff of the Truman Library, especially Liz Safly and David Clark, were patient in explaining what was and was not available for research and they helped me acquire copies of relevant primary sources. Pauline Testerman also patiently guided me in the selection of photographs. Lewis Gould, the series editor, read numerous chapter drafts and critiqued them in positive and insightful ways. I must thank Fred M. Woodward, the patient and inspiring director of the University Press of Kansas, and his remarkable team, notably Larisa Martin and Susan Schott.

I appreciate the financial support of Sterling College in providing me a research grant from the office of President Bruce Douglas. I was also very fortunate to have my own personal editor, my late mother, Margaret, who read each chapter and helped in the revisions of the text. Final responsibility for the contents of this book is, of course, my own.

BESS WALLACE TRUMAN

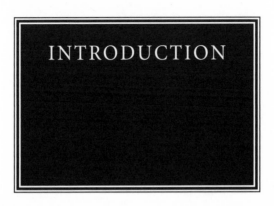

INTRODUCTION

My interest in Bess Truman began when I was a doctoral student studying the presidency of Harry S. Truman. I often asked myself whether she had a role in the Truman White House other than that of the traditional role of hostess. I had read with interest Margaret Truman's official biography of her mother, *Bess W. Truman*, and learned of the strong Truman partnership, but I questioned why a scholar had not produced a book on Mrs. Truman. Three years ago, when I inquired with the University Press of Kansas about the Modern First Ladies series, I was told they needed a scholarly study done on the first lady, and I accepted the challenge. Although Bess Truman left no personal papers, I discovered through my research that there were quite enough sources for a book-length manuscript. The end result is the first book about Mrs. Truman written by a historian. I have found Bess Truman to be a private, intelligent, and influential first lady.

In the postwar years, a female dominion existed in the mostly male process of policy making. It was created by the dogged determination of middle-class white women reformers. Their dominion was a continuation of female reform activity since the Progressive era. Female policy-making bodies first emerged during the New Deal from the unique needs of women who were seeking channels to professionalism. For many women during the New Deal and the immediate postwar years, professionalization sustained reforming commitments.[1] From 1933 to 1953, many women were successful in obtaining federal and state government positions. Bess Truman's activities and agendas as first lady reflected this change in postwar gender roles. After Harry S. Truman was elected president in 1948, Mrs. Truman played a major role in broadening opportunities for women in the federal government. Throughout his administration, she was more of a sponsor of good works than many have realized; she worked closely with voluntary women's organizations such as the Girl Scouts and PEO Sisterhood.

Mrs. Truman's contemporaries have described her as loyal, motherly, good-natured, and athletic. E. Clifton Daniel, her son-in-law, recalled: "I had never seen a family that seemed to be so intensely loyal to each other. Mrs. Truman doesn't express her loyalty quite so trenchantly, let's say, as President Truman does, but she certainly shares in it."[2] Katie Louchheim, vice chair of the Democratic National Committee, noted: "I had such affection, respect, and admiration for her. I would have liked to have been her daughter. . . . I felt that woman had real greatness. Magnanimity was one of her qualities."[3] Dr. Wallace H. Graham, White House physician, remembered: "I was able to get many a laugh out of Mrs. Truman. . . . She did have a fine sense of humor. She always appeared to be a little cold and austere, but she actually wasn't. She was very sentimental."[4] Mary Paxton Keeley, a lifelong friend from Independence, Missouri, remarked on Bess Truman as an athlete: "She was an athlete, really, and she was a crack tennis player. . . . I said, when she was in the White House, 'How in the world could you shake hands with all those people?' And she said, 'It was my tennis arm.' "[5]

Bess Truman was sixty years old when her husband became president. Her values and lifestyle were already set; she knew who she was, and she had little inclination to change. As the product of a small-town aristocracy with nineteenth-century manners and morals, she was repelled by personal publicity, even after ten years as a senator's wife and eighty-three days as the wife of the vice president. A woman's place in public, noted Mrs. Truman, was to "sit beside her husband, be silent and be sure her hat is on straight." The suddenness with which Harry S. Truman was propelled into the presidency by the death of Franklin D. Roosevelt on 12 April 1945 was traumatic for him and for Bess.

Mrs. Truman's predecessor had been not only a dynamic force in American politics but also a renowned world figure. In her twelve years as first lady, Eleanor Roosevelt had traveled across America as her husband's eyes and ears. She had also promoted controversial public projects and causes, written a syndicated column, and given lectures, press conferences, and interviews. That was not a position that Bess Truman was equipped for or aspired to. As a very private person, she was repelled by the thought of giving interviews, and not a little frightened at the idea of holding press conferences.

Bess confided her apprehension to Frances Perkins, the secretary of labor, on the train returning from the Roosevelt funeral at Hyde Park, New York. In relating the incident for the Columbia University Oral History Project, Perkins recalled that Mrs. Truman was "very emotional." She was "all wrought up over the funeral and felt awfully about Roosevelt's death." She was also very worried about stepping into Mrs. Roosevelt's shoes. "I don't know what I am going to do," Mrs. Truman said to Perkins. Mrs. Roosevelt, she said, had suggested that she hold a press conference on the following Tuesday and offered "to sit with me and sort of introduce the girls to me and get me familiar with the procedure. Do you think I ought to see the press?" Perkins replied, "No, Mrs. Truman, I don't think you ought to feel the slightest obligation to do it. . . . I don't think any other first lady did it."[6] Mrs. Truman was emotionally relieved, and thereafter decided she would not try to emulate her successor. Women reporters, whose jobs had been made more secure by Eleanor Roosevelt's press conferences, prodded and criticized the new first lady, but Bess Truman could not be budged.

The Trumans—Harry, Bess, and their daughter, Margaret—were a close family. They cared about each other's opinions. They also enjoyed each other's company and spent many hours together in the White House. The White House staff called them "the Three Musketeers." Harry and Margaret played the piano together, and Bess and Margaret played ping-pong and bridge with mutual friends. All three watched movies in the White House theater, or simply sat and read. There was also a lot of teasing and joking among them; they once surprised a White House butler who entered the family dining room while they were pelting one another with watermelon seeds.

In public, however, Bess Truman not only was reticent, but genuinely shy. She stayed in the background and out of the limelight so much that after she had been first lady for eight months, she could still do her Christmas shopping in Washington's department stores without being recognized.

The contrast between Mrs. Roosevelt and Mrs. Truman as first lady camouflaged the latter's knowledge of political affairs and her influence on her husband and his presidency. Scholars have swung in recent years from considering her contribution insignificant to the other extreme of crediting her as the mastermind behind some of her husband's major policies.

There have been several interpretations of Mrs. Truman since her death, beginning with Margaret Truman's official biography, *Bess W. Truman* (1986). It provided a revealing, behind-the-scenes view of her mother: a gracious but no-nonsense first lady who emphasized family privacy. Chronicling Bess Truman's ninety-seven years, the work is an intimate biography of an extraordinary American woman. Jhan Robbins's earlier portrayal of Mrs. Truman in *Bess and Harry* (1980) depicted her as an activist and political first lady who played a vital role in the Truman partnership and Harry S. Truman's presidency.

Maurine H. Beasley's biographical essay on Mrs. Truman in *First Ladies: Their Lives and Their Legacy* (2001) reveals that Bess Truman personified the ongoing tradition in American political life: the ideal companion for a president by presenting herself as an honest and warm individual who acted as a mother figure for the nation.

Margot Ford McMillan and Heather Roberson provided a chapter analysis of Mrs. Truman's life and first ladyship in *Into the Spotlight: Four Missouri Women* (2004). They believe that although Bess Truman was a reluctant first lady, she was efficient and hardworking. Mrs. Truman, they point out, was determined not to allow the sheer number of people she knew to compromise the quality of her relationships. She often remarked that new arrivals in Washington came down with "Potomac fever," an illness characterized by self-importance and snobbery—an illness Bess Truman was determined she would never catch.

Raymond Frey's essay, "Bess W. Truman: The Reluctant First Lady," in *The Presidential Companion: Readings on the First Ladies* (2006), provides an interpretation of the hidden-hand first lady.

Unlike Eleanor Roosevelt, Mrs. Truman preferred to remain in the background. She would see her most important role as being the president's sounding board and confidante. Frey believes "there is no doubt that she was the most important person in Harry Truman's life, and she was his trusted advisor in private."

Bess Truman was the last president's wife to escape the coverage of television cameras, but she was at the mercy of still cameras, and she was not photogenic. She was a short, plump, matronly woman with gray hair, which, for a time, she wore in the short, curly poodle cut then popular. She was always meticulously groomed, usually in the boxy, tailored suits that were in vogue, with matching hat and gloves. She also did not like to be photographed. And when she was, the results usually confirmed her critics' image of her as rigid and stony-faced.

Although reserved, Bess Truman was good-natured, with a warm, winning manner and a sharp, dry sense of humor. There were other interesting facets to her personality. She had grown up with three younger brothers who had to be beaten at baseball and whistling through one's teeth. She had excelled at most sports, and she remained an avid baseball fan all her life. She attended the games of the Washington Senators whenever she could, and when she could not, she listened to their radio broadcasts. For years after she returned to Independence, she rarely missed an opening game for the Kansas City Royals. She said that she could hardly forgive Margaret for picking the start of baseball season, 21 April 1956, to be married, "where there were 364 other days in the year."

Although Bess may have been a tomboy in her youth, there was never any doubt that she grew up to be a lady. Her mother, Madge Gates Wallace, with whom she lived all of her life until Mrs. Wallace's death in the White House in December 1952, had seen to that. Mrs. Wallace was once described as "the queenliest woman Independence ever produced." Her daughter inherited her personal dignity, though not her imperiousness.

Bess's deeply rooted sense of what was fitting and proper set her on a not-too-successful campaign to curb her husband's salty language. It seemed to the White House staff that her most commonly used expression was, "You didn't need to say that." It was not that Bess was shocked by cusswords. As one of her brothers once pointed out, she had heard them all her life and "even knew how to use them," but she thought they had no place in presidential discourse. Mrs. Truman not only thought her husband should uphold the dignity of the presidency, but also knew he would be hurt if he did not.

Presidents have paid tribute to their wives' influence while stopping short of crediting their advice in any specific way. Harry S. Truman was no exception. But he went as far as was generally acceptable when he said that Mrs. Truman was "a full partner," and that he discussed every decision with her.

Robert F. Kennedy once commented that Jacqueline Kennedy was not the kind of wife who would greet her husband on his return from the Oval Office with "What's new in Laos?" But that is just the kind of question Bess Truman was apt to ask her husband. She took a keen interest in his daily problems, and President Truman respected her judgment. She had worked with him during his years in the Senate and was a paid member of his staff when he was chairman of the Senate Special Committee to Investigate the Defense Program, or the Truman Committee. When Truman was running for vice president, he came under fire for having his wife on his payroll. His reply was, "She earns every cent of it. I never make a speech without going over it with her, and I never make any decision unless she is in on it."[7]

In the White House, he invariably brought work back with him from the Oval Office, and after dinner, Bess would join him in his study. Charles S. Murphy, special counsel to the president, very likely put the matter of Bess Truman's influence in perspective when he said, "The president did not hold up a decision to consult his wife. On the other hand, she had a lot to do with the shape of his attitude about things and people."[8]

Bess Truman's opposition was an important factor in President Truman's decision not to run for reelection in 1952. She had been with him through rough times in his second term, which had included the rise of McCarthyism and the outbreak of the Korean War, and which had been filled with political bitterness and unrelenting partisan attacks on the president.

She had seen President Roosevelt die in office, and she worried about the effect another term would have on her husband's health.

Adding to her apprehension had been an attempted assassination, when two Puerto Rican nationalists tried to shoot their way into Blair House, where the Trumans were living during the renovation of the White House. When President Truman finally announced at a Jefferson-Jackson Day dinner in Washington that he would not run again, Mrs. Truman, sitting at the head table, tried not to show her feelings, but was not completely successful. "When you made your announcement," Major General Harry H. Vaughan, one of the president's poker-playing friends, reported back, "Mrs. Truman looked the way you do when you draw four aces."

Bess Truman returned to Independence little changed from the woman who had gone to Washington as a senator's wife seventeen years earlier. She still saw to it that her house was spotlessly clean; she looked after the household budget; and she did her own shopping, had her Tuesday Bridge Club in, answered all of her own mail, listened to baseball games on the radio, read innumerable mystery novels, and looked after her husband.

Very likely because she had objected to his running for a third term, Bess and Harry had another twenty years together before his death in December 1972, when he was eighty-eight and she was eighty-seven. Bess buried her husband in the courtyard of the Truman Library. "I would like to be buried out here," he once told her, "so that I can get up and walk to my office if I want to. And when the time comes, you'll be there beside me, probably saying, 'Harry, you oughtn't!'"

CHAPTER 1

LADY FROM INDEPENDENCE

It was a hot and humid afternoon on 21 July 1944, inside Chicago Stadium, the site of the Democratic National Convention. Delegates were preparing to cast a second ballot for their vice presidential nominee. Mrs. Truman was seated in a box with her daughter, Margaret, behind the podium. Three days before the convention opened, Senator Harry S. Truman had been informed that he was President Franklin D. Roosevelt's first choice to be his running mate, replacing the more liberal Vice President Henry Wallace. The roll call of states lasted for several hours through the late afternoon and evening, but when Massachusetts declared that it had changed its vote for Truman, assuring him the nomination, the tension in Bess's face disappeared and she smiled. The organist launched into "Happy Days Are Here Again," the Democratic Party's theme song since 1932, and a wave of clapping and whistling delegates rose to their feet to chant "Truman, Truman." For a few minutes, Bess Truman felt happy and proud for her husband, but these feelings soon dissolved into feelings of uncertainty and uneasiness. Rumors had circulated that Roosevelt's physical health was failing, and Bess worried that Harry might one day succeed him. She had no desire to see her husband become president, and she definitely had no wish to become first lady.

Illinois added another fifty-five votes for the senator from Missouri, and more states followed. At 8:14 P.M., the victory was announced, with Truman receiving 1,031 votes over Wallace's 105. Senator Truman gave a one-minute acceptance speech. As soon as he finished, while the delegates cheered, he fought his way off the platform and, with a police escort, made it to the box where Bess and Margaret were sitting. The crowd surged around them as Bess tried desperately to reach him. After several tries, the three Trumans locked arms and slowly made their way to a waiting limousine. Once safely inside, Bess turned to Harry and in a firm voice asked, "Are we going to have to go through this for the rest of our lives?"[1]

A few days later, in Independence, Missouri, three thousand people gathered on the back lawn at 219 North Delaware to congratulate the nominee. Mrs. Truman stood beside her husband under a blooming rose arbor. She greeted each well-wisher who stood in line to shake hands with the senator. The tension, crowds, and public pressure that she had experienced in Chicago were gone but not forgotten. Nevertheless, Bess was relieved to be back home among the people of Independence. Her fourteen-room Queen Anne Victorian home, known by townspeople as the Gates mansion, shaded the lawn. Bess's maternal grandfather, George Porterfield Gates, had been one of the wealthiest citizens of Independence. Gates built the home in the 1880s as a symbol of his wealth. He was co-owner of the Waggoner-Gates Milling Company, which manufactured Queen of the Pantry flour, sold throughout the country as "the finest biscuit and cake flour in the world."[2]

When Mrs. Truman was in Independence, she was recognized as a member of the genteel upper class. Her family had lived there for five generations. Born in Independence on 13 February 1885, Elizabeth Virginia Wallace was raised to be a lady by late nineteenth-century standards. Her parents, David Willock Wallace and Margaret "Madge" Gates Wallace, were married on 13 June 1883. Bessie, as her mother called her, was the oldest of five children. She had three younger brothers: George Porterfield Wallace, born in 1882; Frank Gates Wallace, born in 1887; and David Frederick Wallace, born in 1900. A sister died in infancy, leaving Bessie the only girl in the family. Because she was George Porterfield Gates's first grandchild, Bessie was guaranteed special affection from her grandfather and his wife, Elizabeth. Gates often bounced her on his knee and talked nonsense to her. Bessie's paternal grandfather had died eight years before she was born, but her paternal grandmother, Virginia Willock Wallace, loved her very much. A gifted seamstress, she gave Bessie beautiful handmade silk dresses. The Wallaces had been one of the first families to settle Independence, arriving from Kentucky in 1833, thirty-three years before the Gates family left Illinois for Missouri.[3]

In the mid-nineteenth century, Independence was known as the Queen of the Trails, a lively town where pioneer families joined wagon companies that were westbound on the Santa Fe, California, and Oregon trails. By the 1880s, it had become a placid county seat of Jackson County, Missouri, with a population of 3,500 residents. Strongly Democratic, the people of Independence still held resentments from the Civil War, when Union forces had sacked the area to combat Southern guerrillas. Located ten miles east of Kansas City, the town became a suburb soon after Bess Wallace was born. It offered residents two doctors and a dentist, and it provided stores, saloons, offices, and banks around the courthouse on the town square. The streets of Independence were lined with tall elm and maple trees, and North Delaware Street was one of the most fashionable addresses in town.

With her bright blue eyes and golden hair, Bessie favored her father. She also inherited his good humor and outgoing personality. David Wallace was tall and handsome, with a blond mustache and sideburns. The son of Benjamin Wallace, a former mayor of Independence and member of the state legislature, David Wallace, at age eighteen, had been appointed deputy recorder of marriage licenses in Independence. George Porterfield Gates feared that the dapper twenty-three-year-old Wallace would be unable to support his twenty-one-year-old bride. As it turned out, Gates's assumption was correct.[4]

Madge Gates Wallace was dark-eyed and petite. She had been raised to believe that a woman belonged in the home. The doctrine of separate spheres had become widely accepted for women of means in the early and mid-nineteenth century, and it dictated that the income-earning husband venture forth into the world while the woman stayed home. Domestic life fell completely under female control. Thus, women were expected to devote themselves entirely to private life, leaving their husbands to provide for the household.

Madge, who had been raised with wealth, was called "queenly" by the townspeople of Independence.[5]

The Wallaces lived in a comfortable house on Ruby Street in Independence, where Bessie was born. Within a few years, Wallace mortgaged the house for a $700 loan, but he was able to sell it for a profit when Bessie was two. The family then moved to 608 North Delaware Street, only two blocks from the Gates mansion, which served as a second home to Bessie.[6]

In 1888, David Wallace won election as treasurer of Jackson County. He was reelected two years later. However, party squabbling kept him off the ballot in 1892. In 1893, after being without work for nearly a year, he secured an appointment as deputy U.S. surveyor of customs for the port of Kansas City. The position paid $1,200, a good salary for 1894, but not enough to support a growing family and an extravagant wife. Wallace eventually became mired in debt. He also began to spend more amounts of time at a saloon on the town square. His drinking companions would carry him home and leave him on the front porch instead of sobering him up to meet his wife. Madge Wallace, however, refused to acknowledge that he was an alcoholic.[7]

Except for her father's problems, Bessie led a peaceful and contented childhood, attending public school in Independence and making friends easily. Twenty-seven children lived on North Delaware Street, and Bessie developed several close relationships, especially with Mary Paxton, who lived next door. Mary Paxton, later Keeley, became the first woman graduate of the University of Missouri School of Journalism. Bessie and Mary were lifelong friends.

Mary wrote a book about her early memories. As children, they would spend hours making hollyhock ladies, using bonnetlike catalpa blossoms for heads and pink and red hollyhocks for skirts. They also fished for crawdads with their brothers at MacCauley Pasture, a shady woodland at the end of North Delaware Street. In the summers, as the children on North Delaware Street grew older, the young people held weekend parties, with Japanese lanterns strung across backyards. They had ice cream and mints for refreshments. In the winters, they played card games like hearts and slapjack, or they went ice-skating on moonlit lights on one of the local farm ponds.[8]

Mary Paxton Keeley remembered that Bessie Wallace was one of the best-dressed young women in Independence. The way she wore her party dresses made her stand out at the neighborhood socials. Bessie, like the other girls, wanted to wear longer skirts:

> We all had much the same kind of party dresses, mull with silk sashes, colored or striped, and Bess wore what the rest of us did; the difference was that she always looked more stylish than anyone else we knew. She, like the rest of us, pestered her mother to lengthen her skirts, which were let down gradually; not until we were eighteen were we considered grownup young ladies and then we could wear them full length to the floor like our mothers. . . . Bess always had more stylish hats than the rest of us did, or she wore them with more style.[9]

By the 1890s, the doctrine of the woman's domestic sphere had given way to a more independent woman. The bustle had been banished, and greater numbers of women began to join clubs, play sports, launch careers, and speak in public about a wide variety of issues such as temperance and the right to vote. Bessie Wallace grew up in a world very different from her mother's. Like many young women, Bessie gained self-confidence by participating in sports. She played third base on her brothers' sandlot baseball team and was their home-run champion. From this experience, she developed a lifelong passion for baseball. In high school, she became the best tennis player in Independence. She also excelled at horseback riding and ice-skating. She could whistle through her teeth louder than any boy in Independence, and she could spit watermelon seeds further. By most standards, Bessie was a tomboy.[10]

Although Madge Wallace tolerated her daughter's athletic prowess, she insisted that Bessie learn to be a lady. In high school, Bessie attended Miss Dunlap's Dance Academy with other girls of her age. "We learned the polka and schottische and the Virginia Reel," recalled Mary Paxton Keeley, "but the waltz was the basis, and we mostly danced the waltz and the two-step." Bessie put her dance classes to use at Saturday evening "hops" in local ballrooms and at parties with her friends. One of her friends, Margaret Swope, the niece of wealthy Kansas City real estate developer Thomas Swope, held dances in the ballroom of the Swope mansion in Independence. Bessie would stand with Margaret in the receiving line, a sign of her social status and their friendship.[11]

Bessie's combination of intellect, beauty, social status, and athletic ability made her attractive to potential suitors. Bill Bostian, the postmaster's son, adored her, and he became Bessie's regular tennis partner. Chrisman Swope, the second son of Thomas Swope, courted her by taking her on buggy rides. A longtime admirer—Harry S. Truman—also sought her affection. Truman, however, could not afford to attend the same adolescent festivities that Bessie Wallace frequented. He also wore eyeglasses and was teased mercilessly about them. Fearful that he might break his eyeglasses, Truman shied away from sports, preferring instead to read library books and practice the piano.[12]

Five-year-old Bessie Wallace met six-year-old Harry Truman in Sunday school at the First Presbyterian Church in Independence. The Truman family had arrived in Independence in 1890. Harry was born on 8 May 1884, in Lamar, Missouri, a small farm town 120 miles south of Jackson County. His father, John Anderson Truman, was a horse and cattle trader. His mother's family, the Youngs, ran a 600-acre farm near Grandview, Missouri, thirty miles south of Independence. In 1887, the Trumans moved to the Young farm and spent three years there before relocating to Independence. Although they were Baptists, Martha Ellen Truman accepted the invitation of the local Presbyterian minister to send her children to Sunday school.[13]

Harry Truman always insisted that he fell in love with five-year-old Bessie and never stopped loving her. "She had golden curls and the most beautiful blue eyes," Truman wrote in his memoirs. "We went to Sunday school, public school from the fifth grade through high school, graduated in the same class, and marched down life's road together."[14] Because Independence schools seated pupils in alphabetical order, Bessie sat behind Harry in the sixth, seventh, and high school grades. On a few occasions, she let him carry her books home. Both of them were part of a group that gathered for tutoring in Latin at the home of Truman's first cousins, Nellie and Ethel Noland, who also lived on North Delaware Street. Otherwise, the popular Bessie did not show much interest in the bookish, piano-playing Truman, who did not participate in the athletic and outdoor activities that she enjoyed.[15]

Social status and religious affiliation also affected the early relationship between Bessie Wallace and Harry Truman. He was the son of a livestock trader and a Baptist—an inappropriate combination in Independence's rigid social hierarchy. Mary Paxton Keeley noted that in the hierarchy of church membership, the Presbyterians and Episcopalians were at the top, followed by the Campbellites (Disciples of Christ), the Methodists, and the Lutherans. Farther down were the Baptists, Catholics, and Mormons. The Wallaces had become Episcopalians. "We did not know Baptists or Methodists or Lutherans," Mary Paxton Keeley remembered. "As I look back, it was a snobbish little town."[16]

Bessie was an excellent student. She and Harry Truman both graduated in 1901 from Independence High School. She might have been sent to college had it not been for her father's financial problems. In 1901, David Wallace was two years behind on his property taxes, and he feared that his house would be sold by the county collector. Wallace, unable to manage, turned to his father-in-law for assistance. Madge Wallace offered no comfort, believing that what happened in a "man's sphere" was none of his wife's business.[17]

Forty-three-year-old David Wallace sank deeper into debt, and he became severely depressed. On 17 June 1903, he awoke at dawn, took a revolver from a desk in the bedroom, walked to the bathroom down the hall, and shot himself to death. Eighteen-year-old Bessie sat up in her bed, trembling, when she heard the shot. She could hear her brother, Frank, running down the hall, crying, "Papa's shot himself." When Mary Paxton's father told her about the suicide, she checked on Bessie. "She was walking up and down at the back of the house with clenched hands," Mary remembered. "There wasn't anything I could say, but I just walked up and down with her."[18] Madge Wallace was grief-stricken, and she considered her husband's death a disgrace. In 1903, suicide was a dreadful stigma for a family. To make matters worse, two days later, the local newspaper published a front-page story of Wallace's death. Madge "just went to pieces," said one member of the family, and she became a recluse.[19]

Bessie Wallace's carefree and happy adolescence ended the day that her father tragically took his life. She immediately took charge of her three young brothers and her fragile mother. Although the Gates family assumed financial responsibility for the Wallaces, Bessie became the family leader—a role she held for many years. She also became more private, emotionally controlled, and pessimistic.

The Wallaces soon left Independence for a yearlong retreat in Colorado Springs, Colorado. During those twelve months, Bessie struggled to understand her father's suicide. An intelligent and observant young woman, she began to question her mother's love for her father. She reached the conclusion that her mother's way of loving him had been the passive, mindless love of a genteel lady, and it had been a mistake. She vowed that when she married, she would share her husband's whole life, both the good and the bad. During that year, Bessie came to reject the doctrine of women's and men's separate spheres.[20]

When the Wallaces returned to Independence, they moved into the Gates mansion at 219 North Delaware Street. In 1905, Bessie enrolled at the Barstow School in Kansas City, founded by Wellesley graduate Mary Barstow in 1884. Barstow was an elite school that offered both college preparatory and finishing school courses for young women. She spent a year at Barstow. During this time, she shortened her name to Bess. She did well at the school, earning an A+ in literature and A's in her French and rhetoric classes. Bess also became the star forward on the basketball team, and she won the shot put in a spring track meet. At the end of the year, she did not go to a women's college back East like many of her classmates. Instead, she went home to Independence and resumed her role as head of the Wallace family.[21]

Sadly, Madge Wallace began to retreat from the world around her. Bess, however, did not become a recluse. She joined the Needlework Guild, which made clothes for the poor, as well as a cultural study club. She also organized a bridge club made up of her friends from high school and Barstow. She continued to play tennis and ride horses. Two new friends from Barstow, Agnes and Laura Salisbury, whose father owned a 600-acre farm on the outskirts of Independence, had enough horses to make the North Delaware Street crowd look like a cavalry troop.[22]

One evening in the summer of 1910, Harry Truman rang the doorbell at 219 North Delaware. Bess opened the door and found him with a broad smile and a cake plate in hand. Madge Wallace had baked a cake for Harry's cousins, the Nolands, and they had asked him to return the plate. He jumped at the chance. Bess had not seen or heard from him in nine years since they had graduated from high school. Truman had changed considerably. He stood erect, his skin was deeply tanned, and he had gained weight and muscle. Bess invited Harry to come in, and she led him to the Gates parlor. The beginning of a nine-year courtship took place that summer night.[23]

Madge Wallace was not impressed with Truman, and she did not hide her disapproval. Janey Chiles, a former Independence schoolteacher, recalled, "I thought they would never get married. There wasn't anybody in town Mrs. Wallace didn't look down on. And Harry Truman was not at the time a very promising prospect."[24] Truman's grandfather, Solomon Young, had died, and he and his father were running the Young farm in Grandview. Before returning to the farm, Truman had held a few town jobs that Madge Wallace also thought held no future. After he graduated from high school, he went to work in the mail room of the *Kansas City Star*, but he quit to become a timekeeper on the Santa Fe line. In 1903, Truman was hired as a bank teller for the National Bank of Commerce in Kansas City. The following year, he left for a rival bank, the Union National. He worked as a teller for more than two years until he gave it up to return to the farm.[25]

Every Saturday evening, Truman would travel to Independence by train and streetcar. He would usually bring Bess a small bouquet of roses and violets. "A standard dating custom in Independence," recalled Ethel Noland, "was to take long hikes in the woods. There were many wonderful trails nearby, and Harry and Bess covered them all." They also frequently went fishing along the banks of the Little Blue River. Bess was the angler. She dropped the bait and watched the bobbing cork while Harry sat on the bank and read to her. On Sunday morning, they attended services at the Trinity Episcopal Church in Independence.[26]

Harry sent Bess hundreds of letters from the farm in Grandview. In a letter dated 22 June 1911, he proposed marriage. Three days later, Bess telephoned him and turned him down. She was gentle and considerate. She told him that she hoped they would continue to be friends. Truman replied with another letter that said: "You turned me down so easy that I am almost happy anyway. I never was fool enough to think that a girl like you could ever care for a fellow like me but I couldn't help telling you how I felt. . . . I have been so afraid you were not even going to let me be your good friend. To be even in that class is something."[27]

Bess and Harry became secretly engaged in early November 1913. Bess told him that in the two and a half years since she had rejected his marriage proposal, her feelings for him had changed profoundly. Madge Wallace, who took a dim view of any young man interested in her daughter, tried to discourage the attachment. Madge came to view Truman as the farmer who threatened to take her only daughter away from her. She contended that Truman was not good enough for Bess, a view she apparently continued to hold throughout her life. Bess, however, remained strong and saw Harry regularly.[28]

The power of Madge Wallace's influence in the family became apparent when Bess's brothers, Frank and George, married in 1915 and 1916. Madge persuaded her father to give each of them some land behind the Gates mansion. Frank Wallace married Natalie Ott in 1915. George Porterfield Gates gave the newlyweds the eastern half of a 100-foot lot directly behind 219 North Delaware. Their bungalow home at 601 West Van Horn was built the same year. In 1916, George Wallace announced that he would marry May Southern. Gates gave them the western half of the 100-foot lot to build a home. Construction was finished on 605 West Van Horn by the year's end. Bess's youngest brother, Fred, married in 1930 and brought his wife, Christine, to live at the Gates mansion. Frank followed in his grandfather's footsteps in the flour-milling business. George pursued a career with the Jackson County highway department. Fred was trained as an architect, but he never made enough money to be on his own for very long, and like his father, he became an alcoholic. For these reasons, Bess always felt a greater sense of responsibility for her youngest brother.[29]

Not long before Frank and George Wallace married, Harry Truman bought a 1911 Stafford automobile that allowed him to travel to Independence much faster. He began to take Bess and her brothers and their fiancées on picnics in the country. Truman also invested $11,000 of borrowed money in a lead and zinc mine near Commerce, Oklahoma. The mine did not contain enough ore to become profitable, and he gave it up. In late 1916 and early 1917, Truman engaged in another effort to make more money. He became acquainted with an oil wildcatter, David H. Morgan, of Kansas City, and went in with him in a business venture that involved selling oil leases. Bess Wallace had enough faith in Harry Truman to become one of the first investors, borrowing some money from her grandfather Gates. The company put a well down in Kansas. But Truman lost again. When the United States entered World War I, manpower shortages forced the company to dispose of the leases and cease business operations. A few years later, one of the national oil companies drilled deeper and struck oil. Had Truman been able to continue with drilling operations, he would have become a millionaire.[30]

Truman, a member of the National Guard, volunteered for service after the United States entered World War I in 1917. Bess wanted to marry him before he shipped out to France, but he insisted they wait until the war was over. He wrote Bess an emotional letter: "Bess, I'm dead crazy to ask you to marry me before I leave but I'm not going to because I don't think it would be right for me to ask you to tie yourself to a prospective cripple—or a sentiment. . . . Besides, if the war ends happily and I can steal the Russian or German crown jewels, just think what a grand military wedding you can have, get a major general maybe." He left the United States with a photograph of Bess, on which she had written: "Dear Harry, May this photograph bring you safely home again from France."[31]

While Harry was away, Bess devoted much of her time volunteering to sell war bonds. She was assigned to work Blue Township, not far from Independence. She was very successful and was commissioned a "Liberty Soldier" on the ladies' committee of Blue Township that sold $1,780,000 in bonds. She also joined a women's auxiliary made up of wives and fiancées of members of the 129th Field Artillery Regiment, Truman's regiment, and they compared notes on what their men needed during the war. In early 1918, Bess served on an Independence committee that entertained visiting soldiers from Fort Leavenworth, Kansas. The people Bess encountered on the door-to-door bond drives and the women in the auxiliary noticed that she was not afraid to be close and personal. She would listen sympathetically for hours as others told her their wartime sorrows. Her volunteerism ended abruptly when the 1918 Spanish flu struck Independence. The town closed its schools, theaters, and factories in fear of the pandemic, but it spread rapidly. Bess came down with the flu and had an extremely high fever that lasted for weeks. Several times, the family feared she was dying. Her fever finally broke, and she recuperated slowly at 219 North Delaware. However, the illness left her with a partial hearing loss in her left ear.[32]

The German nation finally agreed to an armistice on 11 November 1918. Back in Independence, Bess was awakened at four in the morning by the pealing of church bells. Within minutes, the sounds of honking horns and fire sirens brought everyone into the streets to celebrate. As soon as the war ended, Captain Harry Truman wrote Bess that he would be in New York by Easter. He asked her to meet him in New York and marry him there. She declined, telling him that she wanted to be married in Independence, where her family and friends could share in the celebration.[33]

On 28 June 1919, thirty-four-year-old Bess Wallace and thirty-five-year-old Harry Truman were married in the small Trinity Episcopal Church in Independence. Bess wore a white georgette gown and a wide-brimmed hat made of white faille, and she carried an armful of roses. After the ceremony, they took a short honeymoon to Chicago, Detroit, and Port Huron, Michigan. Years later, Harry would write "Port Huron" on his letters to Bess to remind her of this romantic time together.[34]

After the honeymoon, at Madge Wallace's insistence, the Trumans moved into the Gates mansion. Both thought it would be a temporary arrangement, but it turned into their home for the rest of their lives. Bess felt responsible for her mother, especially as Madge's mental and physical health deteriorated. But Madge Wallace was often cruel to Harry Truman and made disparaging remarks about him. To keep peace in the family, Truman saw no point in challenging Madge. Neighbor Susan Chiles remembered, "There just didn't seem to be any way in the world to get along with Mrs. Wallace. Bess put up with her, though, stuck with her through thick and thin."[35]

In late November 1919, Harry Truman opened a haberdashery on the corner of Twelfth and Baltimore streets in downtown Kansas City. His business partner was Eddie Jacobson. Truman and Jacobson had successfully run the regimental canteen at Camp Doniphan,

Oklahoma, before they sailed for Europe. After the war, Jacobson proposed they start a haberdashery that sold men's shirts, ties, hosiery, gloves, belts, and hats. Eddie handled the buying, Harry did the selling, and Bess kept the books. She also was in charge of the advertising. She came up with the idea for a large window sign that read: "For True Value Shop at Truman & Jacobson." At first, Truman & Jacobson did a thriving business. Bess liked working for the store. She also considered Eddie and his wife, Bluma, close friends. During this time, Captain Truman was on reserve duty, and the Jacobsons would always include Bess in their trips to Fort Leavenworth to see him.[36] However, Madge Wallace would not allow the Jacobsons to visit at 219 North Delaware. They were Jewish, and to have them in the house would have been a breach of Madge's rigid social code. Apparently, Bess never seriously questioned her mother's anti-Semitism.[37]

Harry Truman's bad luck with business continued. In 1921, the bottom fell out of the nation's economy, and the Truman & Jacobson $40,000 inventory dropped in value to $10,000. Fewer men could afford silk shirts and accessories, and business declined. The store closed that year. Truman narrowly avoided bankruptcy by agreeing to pay his share of indebtedness gradually. "The Trumans never threw money around," Ethel Noland recalled. "But after the store's collapse, they lived more frugally than ever. They skimped for the next fifteen years to pay off outstanding bills." Bess immediately became the family's money manager, cutting back on unnecessary expenses, and helping her husband satisfy his creditors.[38]

Truman was not unemployed for long. In July or August 1921, he began a new profession—the profession of politics. As he stood behind the cash register of the empty haberdashery, he happened to look out the front door and see the Locomobile of Michael J. Pendergast, political boss of eastern Jackson County and brother of Thomas J. Pendergast, the political boss of Kansas City. Accompanying him was his son, Jim, who had been an officer in the 129th Field Artillery. The Pendergasts entered the store and asked Captain Harry to run for eastern judge of the county. Truman accepted the offer. His association with the Pendergast machine ended when the organization collapsed after Tom Pendergast was sent to federal prison in 1939 for income tax evasion.[39]

Bess had some reservations about her husband entering politics, largely because she knew that he was being supported by a corrupt political machine. Moreover, she always believed that her father's lack of success in politics contributed to his alcoholism, depression, and suicide, and she remembered the publicity and public humiliation to which the press had subjected her family after his death. In spite of her trepidation, Bess supported Harry's decision to run for public office. She knew he would be a fair and honest politician who would understand the concerns of the ordinary person. Bess's family connections were also an asset for Truman. In the 1922 campaign, he had the support of the *Independence Examiner*, partially because its editor in chief, William Southern, was the father of Bess's sister-in-law, May Wallace.

Truman was elected county judge of the eastern district of Jackson County in 1922. It was not a judicial position under the Missouri system but rather a two-year administrative one, equivalent to a county commissioner. In January 1923, Judge Truman was sworn into office. He planned to accomplish a great deal during his two years in office, and he discussed his course of action with Bess—a habit he followed for the remainder of his life. Bess thought that Jackson County's road system needed improvement. Together, they drove over every inch of the muddy and badly worn roads. Truman took her advice and hired a new county engineer to oversee road improvements. In 1928 and 1931, he received Tom Pendergast's permission to propose two large bond issues for new road construction that eventually paved every major and secondary road in Jackson County. Bess also accompanied her husband on a visit to see the Jackson County Old Folks Home. She listened to the elderly residents as they told her of the deplorable living conditions, poor sanitation, and poor food that the home provided. After the visit, she recommended that he order a thorough investigation of the institution. He did, and it led to a complete refurbishing of the Old Folks Home as well as the hiring of a new manager and staff. Several years later, the home was singled out as a model for the entire state.[40]

While Truman was involved in county politics, Bess maintained a delicate balance between handling his public relations and staying out of the limelight as much as possible. She read his mail, took his calls, and kept track of the most problematic county issues. She learned every political, legal, and social aspect of his job and became his primary advisor in these matters. She also read the newspaper to see how the public viewed his programs and activities. But she was very sensitive to public criticisms of her close political relationship with her husband. Bess simply did not want it to appear that Truman's wife was helping him make decisions, and she guarded against this perception.

Bess also avoided making public appearances at this time because she was concerned about her health and the health of a future child. She had experienced two miscarriages, the first in 1920 and a second in 1922, and she began to wonder if she had waited too late to have children. Doctors had advised her not to become involved in political rallies and other public events that could cause undue stress on a pregnancy. When she became pregnant again in 1923, she did everything to avoid anxiety, excusing herself from Truman's 1924 reelection campaign. Because of conflicts in the Democratic Party, Harry lost the election, but the Trumans were ecstatic when their first child was born on 17 February 1924. Bess gave birth to Mary Margaret Truman in an upstairs bedroom at 219 North Delaware and made a bed for her in a bureau drawer. After the first two miscarriages, she had refused to buy any baby furniture, for fear of jinxing the pregnancy.[41]

In 1926, the Pendergast machine offered Harry Truman the nomination for presiding judge of the county court. After consulting with Bess, he accepted the offer. The salary was modest, but this was an important decision, and they both knew it. The position came with a great deal of authority, and if Truman won the election, he would have an opportunity to do great things for Jackson County. During the campaign, he took Bess along to meetings and speaking engagements, but she remained aloof. However, behind the scenes, Bess aided and protected her husband's reputation. Her handling of a small political crisis during the campaign illustrates her political astuteness. Truman ran unopposed in the Democratic Party primary. A local attorney, J. Allen Prewitt, a political outsider, wanted Truman to join a committee he had formed for the visit of a St. Louis candidate for the U.S. Senate, Henry B. Hawes. However, Truman was away on army reserve duty, so Bess took over. "I'm afraid Mr. Hawes won't get very far under his [Truman's] patronage," Bess told Prewitt. When word of Bess's remarks reached Tom Pendergast, she was warned that "Mr. Pendergast considered it best for you to keep out of all fights." Bess telephoned Prewitt and told him that Lieutenant Colonel Truman would not be home for another week (a whopping lie), so he could be of no help to his committee.[42]

Truman easily won the August 1926 primary and the general election in November. Bess was now a professional politician's wife. She considered herself an equal partner, and she became her husband's eyes and ears when he was away on guard reserve duty. During his summer tour of duty in 1927, Bess kept Harry informed of politics in Jackson County, sending him clippings of the *Kansas City Star,* visiting his office, and fielding phone calls. Publicly, however, she was more subdued. She became a charter member of the Tuesday Bridge Club in Independence, a group of eleven women who met every Tuesday to play bridge and socialize, and she also served as secretary of the Needlework Guild. That was quite enough for Bess. Her family was her life, and beyond assisting Harry in his job, she had no desire for public attention. The short-lived postsuffrage feminism of the 1920s began to decline in the 1930s, and like many other American women, Bess Truman was content to be a homebound mother.[43]

Bess was relieved of cooking meals for the Wallace–Truman family in 1928, when Madge Wallace employed Vietta Garr, an African American domestic servant. Vietta worked for the Trumans for thirty-five years. In 1951, she accompanied the family to the White House to be a companion to Madge, who had moved to Washington. Vietta knew what foods each of the Trumans enjoyed. She fixed steam-fried chicken or baked Virginia ham, her own special recipe for sweet potatoes, and Bess Truman's favorite, Ozark pudding. Vietta also helped Mrs. Truman raise Margaret from the time the girl was four years old. Margaret called her "Pete," and they developed a strong bond that lasted into Margaret's adulthood.[44] Mrs. Truman treated Vietta like a member of the family. She did not view her as being beneath her, as many African American domestic servants were treated in America at that time. Bess was a longtime believer in the equality of races.

As county judge, Harry Truman worked hard for the construction of a modern road system for Jackson County. He also pushed through a badly needed waterworks system, several modern playgrounds for children, and a new county courthouse. Despite his ties to Tom Pendergast, he gained a reputation for honesty and integrity, and he easily won reelection as presiding judge in 1930. Bess urged Judge Truman to make known his accomplishments, and she helped him prepare a booklet entitled *Results of County Planning—Jackson County*. After its distribution, Truman was chosen president of the Greater Kansas City Planning Association and director of the National Conference of City Planning. With Bess's help, he had developed a statewide reputation for government planning.[45]

As the second term of his county judgeship neared its end, Harry and Bess began to think of the next step because it was not customary for a presiding judge to serve more than eight years. Truman wanted to be governor, but Tom Pendergast had another candidate in mind. The Trumans were almost broke. They did not have enough money to make a payment on their debts from the ill-fated haberdashery business. Then they received some astonishing news: Pendergast had chosen Truman to run for the U.S. Senate. Bess supported her husband's decision to accept the nomination, but she was troubled. She did not want to live in Washington, and she was not sure whether she could endure the personal and political attacks. For example, Truman was called "Pendergast's office boy" by one opponent. Bess would quickly learn that smear tactics and the lies and innuendos published in the press were the hardest part of being a politician's wife.[46]

Truman waged a tough campaign across the state, often speaking as often as sixteen times a day. Bess would frequently appear with him on the platform. Although she was often invited to give a speech, she would graciously refuse. The nearest thing to a campaign speech she gave was a short statement in Oak Grove, Missouri. When the chairman introduced Bess, she rose, smiled, and said, "You're about to hear from Harry Truman, by far the best man in the race. But then I may be a bit prejudiced since I'm married to him."[47]

Truman won the August primary and enjoyed an overwhelming victory in the November 1934 election. The day after the election, Bess attended her usual Tuesday bridge club. The members were amazed at her calm. An interview the next day with a *Kansas City Star* reporter suggests that she was somewhat hesitant to leave Independence. "Of course I'm thrilled to be going to Washington," Bess said. "But I have spent all my life here on Delaware Street and it will be a change. I was born on Delaware Street and was married to Harry sixteen years ago when he came back from the World War. We never have had or desired another home."[48] Bess would spend the next seventeen years in Washington, but throughout that period, she always regarded Independence as her true home. *Collier's* magazine confirmed: "The wife of the junior senator from Missouri explained that everyone is away from home in Washington. Unquestionably she still regards herself as away from home when she is in the capital, or any place except Independence."[49]

The Trumans rented a furnished five-room apartment from Tilden Gardens, a five-story brick structure at 4701 Connecticut Avenue. Rent cost them $125 a month. Senator Truman earned $10,000 a year, and the family lived modestly. Their only extravagance was a rented piano. Bess did all of the cooking, cleaning, and shopping. When Truman became vice president in 1944, they continued to reside there. At that time, a journalist for the *New York Times* reported, "Mrs. Truman has been a familiar sight in the neighborhood shopping center with her grocery basket, intent upon selecting food for the family."[50] Bess loved to drive her own automobile around Washington for shopping excursions and social events. After Truman was reelected in 1940, he brought her a 1941 dove-gray Chrysler Windsor sedan. She drove the car until 1945. (Her Chrysler is in the custody of the Harry S. Truman Library, and it is often put on museum display.)

From 1935 through 1940, the Trumans were together in Washington each spring. In summer, Bess and Margaret returned to Independence, and in the fall, Margaret enrolled in school there. They went back to Washington when Congress convened, and Margaret enrolled each spring in a private girls' school, Gunston Hall. Bess, however, continued to expand her knowledge of political issues, particularly those affecting Missouri voters. She also made friends with other senators' wives, discovering that many were from small towns and farms. They were easy to meet and know, and after a short time in Washington, Bess had a new circle of friends.[51]

In 1935, Bess Truman met Eleanor Roosevelt. Their meeting was not intimate. Bess was in a group of senatorial wives who had been invited to the White House for tea. Mrs. Roosevelt had emerged as a power in her own right by 1935. She held weekly press conferences, wrote a newspaper column, and traveled thousands of miles on behalf of her husband. Mrs. Truman and the first lady shook hands and exchanged a few words. "Like most Democratic women," wrote Margaret Truman, "Mother admired Eleanor Roosevelt's energy." Bess, however, also wondered how she found time to be a hostess at the White House.[52]

On her trips back to Independence, Bess became a hardworking political observer. She read many Missouri newspapers and talked to neighbors. Carefully gauging the mood of Missouri's voters, she would send Harry Truman newspaper clippings to illustrate trends that she noticed. She also read the *Congressional Record* and analyzed the proceedings of Congress for her husband. Bess's daily correspondence from Missouri helped Senator Truman stay accountable to Missouri voters. She also warned him that Tom Pendergast's power was fading. In 1939, Pendergast pleaded guilty to bribery and income tax evasion. Truman was up for reelection in 1940, and Governor Lloyd Stark, a political opportunist, announced that he would challenge him in the Democratic primary. District Attorney Maurice Milligan, the Pendergast prosecutor, also declared his candidacy.[53]

To make political matters more difficult, President Franklin D. Roosevelt concluded that Truman's chances at reelection were slim, and he allied himself with the governor. Senator Truman received a telephone call from Roosevelt's secretary, Steve Early, the day before the deadline for filing for the senatorial race. The president offered him a lifetime appointment on the Interstate Commerce Commission. Harry Truman consulted his closest advisor—Bess Truman—and together they decided that he should decline the appointment and file for reelection. Bess immediately came to dislike President Roosevelt for his political maneuvering. Margaret Truman concluded: "Bess simply disliked the man for the tricky, inconsistent way he played politics. But she never passed over into that tribe of people who hated the President."[54]

Governor Stark waged a mudslinging campaign. He immediately tore into Truman, calling him a "rubber-stamp senator," a fraud, and a Pendergast lackey. Ethel Noland recalled, "Bess was really het up about that primary. She felt it was the most vicious she had ever seen. That if all the mud slung could be set in piles, they could cover the entire state." In spite of the dirty fighting, Bess counseled Harry to avoid using similar tactics against his two opponents. As a result, the Truman campaign was rather low-key. Cars were decorated with American flags and signs reading "Keep a True Man on the Job—Senator Harry S. Truman" and "Tried and True, That's Truman." Bess was at her husband's side when he visited seventy-five counties in June and July 1940. She shook hands with thousands of Missourians at political rallies, often until her hand ached.[55]

Bess began editing her husband's speeches during the 1940 primary campaign, a practice that she continued through his presidency. She was always pleased when he received loud cheers after giving a speech. Much of her editorial work at that time concentrated on cleaning up Truman's salty language. At one campaign stop, Truman delivered a speech to a Kansas City Grange convention. Bess and a friend were in the audience and heard him use the word *manure* several times. Bess's companion whispered, "Why on earth can't you get Harry to use a more genteel word?" Bess replied, "Good Lord, Helen, it's taken me years to get him to use manure."[56]

The Trumans campaigned hard through the summer of 1940, but it appeared as though the odds were too high to overcome. On 5 August 1940, the night of the primary election, they went to bed with early returns showing Stark in the lead by 11,000 votes. At 3:30 A.M., the phone rang. Bess answered, and a voice on the other end said, "I'd like to congratulate the wife of the senator from Missouri." She was so despondent that she thought it was a joke. "I don't think that's very funny," Bess replied, slamming down the telephone. Later, the Trumans realized that the caller had been the campaign manager in St. Louis. He had good news—Senator Truman was running ahead. When the final votes were counted, Truman received 262,552, Stark had 254,584, and Milligan had only 125,024. The senator went on to win reelection easily in November. He returned to Washington in triumph.[57]

Immediately after Truman's 1940 reelection, Missourians began sending him letters about war profiteering and waste at the state's new army base, Fort Leonard Wood. When he investigated, he found expensive equipment left outside to rust in the rain and hundreds of men collecting a salary for no work. Harry discussed the situation with Bess, and she encouraged him to widen his investigation, even if it meant embarrassing President Roosevelt. She packed his bags and sent him on a trip to military posts across the country. Truman drove 30,000 miles to examine firsthand the operations and conditions of military installations and defense plants. He returned to Washington convinced that something had to be done to eliminate the waste. He took his case to the Senate, which voted unanimously to create the Special Committee to Investigate the National Defense Program, with Senator Truman as chairman.[58]

On 7 December 1941, the Japanese bombed Pearl Harbor. Bess called Harry from Washington to give him the news. He was staying at the Pennant Hotel in Columbia, Missouri, when she woke him. Truman immediately caught a plane for Washington, and Bess called the airline through the night to chart the plane's progress as it headed eastward in terrible weather. She picked him up at the airport in pouring rain and drove him to the Capitol just in time to hear President Roosevelt ask Congress for a declaration of war.[59]

World War II made it even more important that the Truman Committee, as it was called, conduct a sweeping investigation of the national defense industry. The committee's work made Senator Truman a national figure largely because it ended up saving taxpayers over $14 billion. Favorable stories about Truman began appearing in the press. *Time* magazine put him on the cover in 1943 after the Truman Committee's work had been reported. In a poll for *Look* magazine in May 1944, he was named one of the ten most successful public officials in Washington. *Reader's Digest* ran a story about him titled "Billion Dollar Watchdog." *Reader's Digest* was a favorite in Independence, and Bess was happy when members of her bridge club called to say that they had read the article.[60] Truman also spoke regularly on the radio about the committee's findings, and Bess would give him feedback. In 1942, she told him that a recent speech he had given "was the best radio speech I've ever heard you make. . . . In your spare time it really would be a good idea to take a few speech lessons if you are going to be on the radio from now on. But if you keep on doing as well as you did last night you won't need any."[61]

Because Bess had become such an important partner, and because their finances were low, Harry put her on the Senate payroll as an assistant clerk in his office. Her salary was $2,280 a year when she was hired on 1 July 1941. The next year, her salary increased to $4,500. Because his work on the Truman Committee required frequent travel to visit military installations and defense plants, Bess became more involved in the daily operations of the office. She became the principal editor of committee reports and speeches, answered his personal mail, and handled public relations with constituents. In addition to her work in Truman's office, Bess was active in the United Services Organization (USO). She spent at least one day a week at the H Street USO in Washington, helping to prepare and serve lunches.[62] Harry Truman gave Bess Truman full credit for his emergence as a "senator's senator" in Washington. On 27 June 1942, one day before their twenty-third wedding anniversary, he told her: "Thanks to the right kind of a life partner for me we've come out reasonably well. A failure as a farmer, a miner, an oil promoter, and a merchant but finally hit the groove as a public servant—and that due mostly to you and lady luck."[63]

By 1941, Bess Truman had matured from politician's wife to a full political partner. She found fulfillment in her job as her husband's chief clerk. She would often take work home with her, and she was frequently seen at a neighborhood beauty shop, sitting under the dryer, editing speeches and reports with a stubby yellow pencil. She also continued to spend summers in Independence, primarily checking on the welfare of her elderly mother. The days fell into a routine for three years. Then, in the summer of 1944, her comfortable life changed dramatically.[64]

In 1944, President Roosevelt announced that he would run for an unprecedented fourth term. Leaders of the Democratic Party knew that Roosevelt was coming apart physically. They noticed that his weight was dropping; they saw how his hands shook; and they saw the dark circles under his eyes. Party chairman Robert E. Hannegan and others convinced Roosevelt that he needed to replace Vice President Henry Wallace with a more reliable candidate. They recommended either associate justice of the Supreme Court William O. Douglas or Senator Harry S. Truman. By 19 July, on the eve of the Democratic convention, Roosevelt chose Truman as his running mate.[65] When

Truman received the news in Chicago, consternation seized him. He called Tom Evans in Kansas City, a businessman friend of his since the early 1920s. "I need you up here to help keep me from being vice president," Truman told Evans. Arriving in Chicago, Evans questioned Truman why he did not want to be vice president. "Well, I don't want to drag out a lot of skeletons out of the closet," Truman told him. When Evans asked him what skeletons he had, Truman said: "Well, the worst thing is that I've had the boss [Bess] on the payroll in my Senate office and I'm not going to have her name drug over the front pages of the paper and over the radio."[66]

It may be that another skeleton bothered Harry Truman, but he did not mention it to Evans. Bess Truman did not want him to be vice president, or president, because she feared the publicity would reveal her father's suicide. Bess worried what effect press coverage might have on her mother, who was past eighty. Moreover, neither Bess nor Harry had told their daughter, Margaret, about the suicide. However, Margaret has revealed that one of her aunts discussed the matter with her in the summer of 1944. When she inquired of her father, he was furious; he warned Margaret never to mention it to her mother.[67]

A third concern was Bess Truman's general dislike of the White House. She never forgave President Roosevelt for what he had done to her husband in the 1940 primary. In addition, she believed that the publicity that surrounded the White House was bad for the inhabitants. Both she and her husband disliked the divorces of the Roosevelt children and believed that their upbringing at 1600 Pennsylvania Avenue had been partly to blame. Despite the fact that Margaret was twenty and a student at George Washington University in Washington, D.C., Bess Truman wanted to protect her daughter from the glare of publicity.[68]

In the months before the Chicago convention, Mrs. Truman had believed the vice presidential nomination was too remote to be concerned about. Suddenly the reality was at hand. On the afternoon of 19 July, Harry Truman was summoned to a hotel room where the Democratic party leaders were waiting. On the phone they had Roosevelt, who stated, "You tell the Senator that if he wants to break up the Democratic part in the middle of the war, that's his responsibility." With everyone in the room looking at him, Truman responded,

"Well, if that is the situation I'll have to say yes."[69] Bess Truman was not happy about the turn of events, but she stood aside. Later that day, she granted convention reporters a brief interview, where she said, "I'm not very politically inclined and we've never really discussed whether I would campaign with him if he were the nominee."[70]

Truman campaigned tirelessly for Roosevelt in 1944, traveling thousands of miles across the country. Bess announced that she and Margaret would stay in Independence that summer. She also made it clear to her husband that she would not campaign with him on a day-to-day schedule. Bess only made a few appearances at major campaign rallies. Throughout most of the campaign, Mrs. Truman remained obscure, and reporters knew little about her. Early in the campaign, she agreed to one press conference, where she admitted that she was "almost reconciled" to Harry Truman's nomination. When reporters asked her why she had been opposed to it, Bess replied that her reasons were "perhaps selfish." She liked being the wife of a senator, but she disliked the "pressures" she expected would be put on a vice president's wife. Bess then gave the reporters a glimpse of her political partnership with Harry Truman. She said she "understood the [political] issues," but she declined to comment on them, clarifying that that was "the Senator's job." The rest of her remarks dealt with her husband's preferences in food.[71]

Bess Truman was so little known in Washington that the Democratic National Committee wrote an erroneous press release about her. It put out a four-paragraph biographical sketch stating that Mrs. Truman was a former schoolteacher.[72] However, she was briefly thrown into the spotlight when the Republicans probed into Truman's family life. As Harry Truman feared, Bess's job in his Senate office and her salary became an issue.

Republicans charged that Mrs. Truman had been "secretly employed" in Truman's office. Republican congresswoman Clare Booth Luce, wife of wealthy publisher Henry Luce, called Mrs. Truman "Payroll Bess." "Overtime Bess" was another variation.[73] Harry Truman was infuriated; nothing aroused his anger more than attacks directed at his family. Vigorously defending his wife, Truman told reporters it was no secret that Bess was on the Senate payroll. "She's a clerk in my office and does much of my clerical work," he said. "I need her here and that's the reason I've got her there. I never make a report or deliver a speech without her editing it. . . . There's nothing secret about it." The issue was defused when one of Truman's critics, Republican Roy Roberts, managing editor of the *Kansas City Star*, came to Bess Truman's defense. "She earned every penny of it," Roberts wrote. Mrs. Truman received no further scrutiny from the press. To her immense relief, nothing was said about the death of her father.[74]

The Roosevelt–Truman ticket won handily—432 electoral votes to 99 for Thomas E. Dewey—in the November 1944 election. Afterward, the Trumans regrouped in Independence for Christmas. Bess and Margaret spent most of their time in Kansas City, shopping for dresses to wear to the inauguration. Inaugural parties began on 20 December in Washington and lasted until the inauguration on 20 January 1945. Mrs. Truman attended a majority of the parties; she also fed and entertained all of the Wallace and Truman relatives who arrived in Washington for the inauguration.[75] After the ceremony, President Roosevelt retired to an upstairs White House room, leaving his wife and the Trumans to greet 1,800 guests. Speaker of the House Sam Rayburn recalled that as he went through the long receiving line, Bess Truman, who was an avid baseball fan, told him: "I feel like I'm pitching both ends of a double-header."[76] It was an exhausting day for Mrs. Truman, who was only one month away from her sixtieth birthday.

During her husband's ten years in the Senate, Bess Truman had only been known to a small circle of friends. She rarely attended lavish Washington parties. Bess had grown accustomed to Harry bringing home a briefcase of unfinished work. After dinner, they would tackle his pile of papers, discuss the next day's agenda, listen to the radio, and go to bed. But as wife of the vice president, she was required to serve as President Roosevelt's goodwill ambassador. Because the Roosevelts rarely attended outside functions, Washington hostesses invited the Trumans. Perle Mesta and Gwendolyn Cafritz, two of Washington's leading hostesses, adopted them.[77] Vice President Truman would often play the piano at the parties. At one gala, actress Lauren Bacall suddenly jumped on top of Truman's piano and displayed her beautiful legs for photographers. The photographs made all the leading newspapers and magazines. Bess Truman was indignant when she saw them. It was the kind of publicity that she had been worried about. Thereafter, Harry Truman ceased his social piano playing.[78]

Mrs. Truman probably would have been more upset about the Lauren Bacall incident if she had thought that her husband might soon become president. In March 1945, she received a letter from Ethel Noland telling her that a *Boston Globe* reporter had been to Independence gathering information on Harry Truman. The reporter was convinced that President Roosevelt was near death. Bess wrote Ethel Noland: "I hope the Boston Globe man is a mighty bad prognosticator. F.D.[R.] looks fine to me. I sat by him at a W.H. dinner last week and had a good chance for close observation. He's a little deaf—but that's not going to wreck him. So am I! (a little deaf)."[79] Mrs. Truman either observed Roosevelt on one of his good days or she was in a state of denial.

On 12 April 1945, Franklin D. Roosevelt died of a massive brain hemorrhage at Warm Springs, Georgia. Bess Truman was at home, but she did not have the radio on. Her husband called her from the White House and gave her the news. "I'm sending a car for you and Margaret," he told her. "I want you here when I'm sworn in." Bess put down the telephone and began to cry. She made her way down a hall to her daughter's bedroom, sobbing so hard that she could barely speak. Within an hour, the Secret Service drove Bess and Margaret to the White House. After they arrived, Mrs. Truman asked to see Eleanor Roosevelt, and she offered her deepest sympathy. Mrs. Roosevelt thanked her and said, "I just told Harry I am ready to do anything I can to help. That of course applies to you, too." Bess thanked her and hurried to the Cabinet Room, where Cabinet members and congressional leaders had gathered to watch Harry S. Truman sworn in as the thirty-third president.[80]

Frances Perkins, Roosevelt's secretary of labor, witnessed the ceremony, and she recalled Bess Truman's demeanor:

> I remember exactly how she looked that day. She had been crying. She had been weeping, and her eyes were red and swollen, and it was with difficulty that she kept her face straight from contortions of grief during the swearing-in. She's a quickly emotional person, and had naturally cried in her stress and confu-

sion, but she stood there like at Trojan, just startled and having to bear it.[81]

After Roosevelt's funeral, the Trumans moved out of their apartment on Connecticut Avenue to Blair House, across the street from the White House. Bess Truman had insisted that Eleanor Roosevelt be given all the time she needed to move. On 17 April, Mrs. Roosevelt gave Mrs. Truman a tour of the White House and introduced her to the staff. Mrs. Roosevelt mentioned the occasion in her "My Day" newspaper column: "Yesterday I took Mrs. Truman all through the White House. I always have a pride in the beauty of the rooms. . . . It was good to find Mrs. Truman so appreciative of the things that I have loved."[82] The following day, Eleanor Roosevelt came to Blair House to say good-bye and to apologize for the condition of the White House. She had not had the time as first lady to attend to decorating and housekeeping. When the last of twelve trucks loaded with the Roosevelts' belongings left the grounds, Bess Truman closely inspected the White House. Chief Usher J. B. West remembered, "She walked across the street to the White House the day after Mrs. Roosevelt's departure. It was like a ghost house. The walls of the second floor room were streaked with dust and faded around the outlines of Mrs. Roosevelt's pictures. Much of the furniture was shabby, badly in need of an upholsterer. . . . What little was left in the White House gave it the appearance of an abandoned hotel."[83]

Mrs. Truman soon learned that Congress allowed each new administration $50,000 to paint and refurbish the White House. Thus, her first order of business as first lady was to request a thorough cleaning and redecoration of the private quarters before the Trumans moved in. For almost two weeks, she worked with Chief Usher West and a Kansas City decorator, who brought her paint samples and fabric swatches. She personally selected the color scheme for the private quarters and the fabrics for new draperies and upholstery. "For two more weeks the White House staff painted, hung draperies, cleaned, upholstered, and rearranged the White House for the Trumans," recalled J. B. West.[84]

Mrs. Truman's next order of business was to assemble a staff for the East Wing. She hired Reathel Odum, a former bank clerk in St. Louis, who had worked in Truman's Senate office since 1936, to be her personal secretary. Odum had been raised in Benton, Illinois. She spent seventeen years with the Trumans. Odum's oral history provides interesting glimpses of President and Mrs. Truman—for example, how much he missed Bess when she went home to Independence in the summer. "He'd put his head in the office door and say, 'Is there any mail from the Boss? If there isn't, I'm going to fire every one of you,'" Odum recalled. "That was a standing joke." Although Harry had a reputation for salty language, Odum said, "He never did swear in front of us girls. He put women on a pedestal." When asked about Mrs. Truman's role as first lady, Odum remembered, "After meeting so many people and shaking their hands at receptions, she would go to her room and soak her hand in paraffin."[85]

Odum arrived at Truman's Senate office in Washington in October 1936 and worked there until 1945. She and Mrs. Truman volunteered together at the local USO during World War II. "We peeled carrots and did whatever to help entertain soldiers away from home," Odum noted. Often they took bike rides around the Tidal Basin.[86]

In 1947, Odum began accompanying Margaret Truman on her concert tours. Asked how Margaret reacted to music critics, Odum said: "She tried not to read the reviews. She had determination to go ahead despite the critics."[87]

After her White House service, which ended when President Truman left office in 1953, Odum worked as a secretary for Senator Stuart Symington of Missouri, and for the Truman Scholarship Foundation. Whenever the Trumans returned to Washington, she recalled: "I'd go over to the Mayflower and say hello."[88]

Edith Helm became Bess Truman's White House social secretary. She was seventy-one years old. Helm was first hired as social secretary by Edith Wilson and traveled with the Wilsons to the Paris Peace Conference of 1919. She married Admiral James M. Helm in the 1920s and temporarily retired from her White House duties until Eleanor Roosevelt persuaded her to return. Helm headed the nine-person White House social office, and Mrs. Truman relied on her for protocol and handling the press. Helm retired in 1953, and a year later, she wrote her memoir, *The Captains and the Kings,* in which she revealed her experiences in the White House.[89]

Bess Truman proved early on that she was a formidable behind-the-scenes force when it came to East Wing operations. During the Trumans' first week in the White House, the president's new secretary, Eddie McKim, discovered that stenographers were working on thousands of letters that had poured in to Mrs. Roosevelt after her husband's death. McKim fired the women and ordered the work stopped. According to Reathel Odum, when Mrs. Truman heard about it, she asked her husband, "What was Eddie McKim doing over here? We run this ourselves." The next morning the stenographers were back at work on Mrs. Roosevelt's mail.[90]

Even though Mrs. Truman wasted no time breaking away from the activist political role that Eleanor Roosevelt had established, she admired Mrs. Roosevelt, and she corresponded frequently with her predecessor. "I have thought of you so often," Bess wrote Eleanor in late May 1945, "realizing how much you must have to do in sorting out your many belongings and the great accumulation which followed you from here. . . . If you plan to be in Washington at any time I hope you will let me know so that I may see you again. It is something that I always look forward to."[91] Mrs. Roosevelt often visited the Trumans when she was in Washington, and President Truman appointed her the American delegate to the United Nations.

Bess Truman was much more forthright about her true feelings in her letters to Mary Paxton Keeley. One month after she had become first lady, she told Mary, "We are not any of us happy to be where we are but there's nothing to be done about it except to do our best—and forget about the sacrifices and many unpleasant things that bob up."[92]

Mrs. Truman liked being the wife of the senator from Missouri. Harry's 1940 victory had been important to her. After nearly twenty years of political and economic uncertainty, the Trumans had achieved permanence and security. She had looked forward to playing the pleasant role as a senator's wife for the rest of her life. Bess had not wanted Harry to become vice president in 1944. Initially, she had dismissed the idea as a "plot" by Robert Hannegan and other ambitious politicians. And Senator Truman had written Margaret: "Hope I can dodge it. 1600 Pennsylvania is a nice address but I'd rather not move in through the back door—or any other door at sixty."[93]

At that point, Bess could have forced Harry S. Truman to refuse to become a candidate for vice president. She could have told him that the idea of him becoming president and her, first lady was intolerable to her. But there was an invisible line in the Truman partnership that Bess would not cross. She never hesitated to try to influence her husband's decisions. But she never attempted to control him. Thus, she allowed him to accept the inevitability of becoming vice president—and eventually president.

Bess Truman became the first postwar first lady, and as the nation changed, so did her role in the White House. Part of Bess's concept of being a lady was the complete acceptance of responsibility, wanted or unwanted. Although she never desired to be first lady, she accepted the many responsibilities of her position. In doing so, she earned the reputation of being one of the most dedicated and hardworking first ladies. The Truman partnership became stronger during their years in the White House, and her behind-the-scenes influence on her husband also made her one of the most influential first ladies.

CHAPTER 2

BECOMING FIRST LADY

In late May 1945, Bess Wallace Truman stood before three radio microphones, facing a small crowd of naval officers. Behind her were two new navy hospital evacuation airplanes. It was her first public appearance as first lady. The war in Europe had ended, but the United States was still fighting the Japanese. She had accepted an invitation to christen the airplanes. In one hand she held a large, unscored bottle of champagne. In her other hand, she grasped her speech. A group of reporters stood to one side of the crowd with their cameras ready to photograph the christening ceremony. Mrs. Truman smiled, cleared her throat, and spoke into the microphones: "In sending forth these planes we send them with our love and sincere desire that the wounded whom they carry will be brought safely home." She then stepped back and swung the champagne bottle against the front of one of the airplanes. It did not break. Mrs. Truman struck the airplane repeatedly—six times—but the bottle refused to break. Finally a navy lieutenant came forward and struck it with a hammer. The champagne spewed out, soaking the front of Mrs. Truman's dress. It was an embarrassing scene for the first lady, and as a result, she may have decided never to allow herself to be caught in similar circumstances again. No doubt her dislike of publicity was reinforced by the event. She later admitted, "I have no desire to have my voice recorded for posterity."[1]

The botched christening ceremony had been beyond her control, but Bess Truman's initial failure to understand that her social activities carried political overtones led her into another embarrassing incident. She accepted an invitation from the Daughters of the American Revolution (DAR) to attend a tea in her honor at Constitution Hall on 12 October 1945. It then came to light that Hazel Scott, a well-known jazz pianist and wife of Democratic congressman Adam Clayton Powell Jr., was turned down by the DAR to give a concert at Constitution Hall. The DAR racially discriminated against African Americans, and Eleanor Roosevelt had resigned from the organization in 1939 when opera singer Marian Anderson was barred from performing. The day before Mrs. Truman was to attend the tea, Powell sent her a telegram urging her not to attend. "I can assure you," Powell told her, "that no good will be accomplished by attending and much harm will be done. If you believe in 100 percent Americanism, you will publicly denounce the DAR's action."[2]

Bess did not believe in segregation, but she sidestepped the issue and defended her privacy and gentility. Her response to Representative Powell was graceful:

> In acknowledging your telegram of October eleventh, may I call your attention to the fact that the invitation to which you refer was extended and accepted prior to the unfortunate controversy which has arisen. Personally I regret that a conflict has arisen for which I am nowise responsible. In my opinion my acceptance of the hospitality is not related to the merits of the issue which has since arisen. I deplore any action which denies artistic talent an opportunity to express itself because of prejudice against race or origin.[3]

Bess attended the tea, and Powell retaliated by saying, "From now on, Mrs. Truman is the last lady." It was an act of defiance on her part. She did not want a congressman dictating her social life. President Truman backed her and banned Powell from the White House for all events—even for the annual receptions for members of Congress.[4]

African Americans and liberals tried to avoid attacking Mrs. Truman and instead attacked the DAR. Eleanor Roosevelt did not ignore the controversy, but she also did not condemn her successor. In her newspaper column, "My Day," Mrs. Roosevelt mentioned "this recent controversy" and criticized the "agreement among all Theatre owners of the District of Columbia." She called on the DAR to "lead" the "glorious crusade" for desegregation. Many newspapers also covered the story on 12 October, and most treated the Trumans as heroes caught between the DAR's racism and Powell's rabble-rousing. The *Kansas City Star* upheld the DAR's right "to be foolish or narrow" and attacked Powell's behavior as "the type of thing that retards progress toward improving race relations."[5]

Hundreds of letters swamped the White House, and both supporters and critics placed Bess Truman at the heart of the controversy. Many women correspondents believed that Mrs. Truman fulfilled feminine ideals by not politicizing the DAR's position. "We can all feel it unfair to bar great artists from this hall—but feel it most unfair for Cong. Powell to criticize in any way your attending the tea. . . . We are honored to have such a retiring, charming, and homey First Lady," wrote one woman from New York.[6] "You did perfectly right in attending the DAR tea. It's high time we really had a first lady with gumption enough to think for herself and not be the tool of others for political reasons," wrote another.[7]

When her friend, Mary Paxton Keeley, urged her to leave the DAR, Bess refused. "I agree with you that the DAR is dynamite at present but I'm not 'having any' just now," she wrote Mary. "But I was plenty burned up with the wire I had from that ——— in N.Y."[8] Bess was too ladylike to fill in the blank, but her friends and family noticed her indignation. Margaret Truman later wrote: "Much damage was done, not to race relations but to the Truman partnership. There could not have been a worse beginning to her first ladyship, as far as Bess was concerned." President Truman responded by condemning the DAR's refusal to permit Miss Scott to use the hall and stated: "One of the marks of a democracy is its willingness to respect and reward talent without regard to race or religion."[9] In the end, the DAR controversy strengthened Mrs. Truman's desire to avoid the press and escape the White House as often as she could.

Not long after Harry Truman became president, Bess Truman made plans to return to Independence for the summer, just as she always had during his senatorial years. Mrs. Truman hosted nine teas and two garden parties and attended two state dinners in May and early June 1945. Then she and Margaret departed by train for Missouri.[10] Her main reason for leaving Washington was to oversee the renovation of her eighty-year-old home. She had contracted carpenters, painters, and plumbers for the job, and they were scheduled to begin renovations of 219 North Delaware in mid-June. During that time, the exterior of the house was painted white and the press began to refer to it as the Summer White House. The slow pace of the work and the confusion eventually irritated Mrs. Truman. "This house is bedlam and I wish I had never come home," she wrote Reathel Odum. "There is someone working in almost every room in the house and a horde of them on the outside. . . . Vietta came today so that will help. At least I don't have to cook."[11]

In Independence, Mrs. Truman learned that she could not escape public scrutiny. Two hundred townspeople greeted her and Margaret when they arrived at the depot. Hundreds of cars drove slowly by the Summer White House, and hundreds of the curious trooped past the home on foot every day. In late June 1945, President Truman stopped in Independence on his way back from a U.N. conference in San Francisco. He spent four days at home with Bess. She had hoped that it would be a quiet visit, but he brought the presidency with him. It began with a crowd of thousands welcoming him home at the airport. By day three, Bess told Reathel Odum, "The place has been running over with all sorts of people."[12]

Dismayed by the lack of privacy, Bess reacted by declining to be photographed with her husband and daughter. The Associated Press issued an article with the headline, "The First Lady is Determined to Avoid the Limelight," and noted Mrs. Truman's dislike of publicity in her hometown. "Mrs. Truman refused even to pose with her family during President Truman's first homecoming, and the pictures showed only the President and his 21-year-old daughter, Margaret, sitting in lawn chairs," wrote A.P. news editor Charles Nutter.[13] Bess disliked being photographed, and she certainly was not going to pose for reporters who had intruded on the privacy of her home. After this incident, the press learned that Mrs. Truman would not be cooperative when she was in Independence, and they left her alone during her trips back home.

The Secret Service detail assigned to 219 North Delaware also learned a thing or two from Mrs. Truman. Shortly after President Truman left town, she called the two agents in and told them that she knew there might be occasions in Washington where their presence would be required, but anytime she was in Independence, she did not want them trailing her. The agents maintained a detail at the Summer White House through January 1953, but they ceased following the first lady when she did her shopping, chose to go to a luncheon, or attended a meeting of her bridge club.[14]

In early August 1945, Mrs. Truman returned to Washington. On 4 September, she wrote Ethel Noland a letter that indicated she was homesick: "I've been wondering how all of you are. . . . I am getting anxious to go home again. I was sick to miss seeing Chris and Marian but there was nothing I could do about it. . . . The Ambassador of Guatemala and his gal are calling this afternoon so I must get on down there. It's always something."[15] At this time Bess Truman was a reluctant first lady, but as the months passed, she grew more accustomed to her position, and she developed an active agenda as hostess and club woman.

It took Mrs. Truman several months to warm up to the press and the public. Women reporters, whose jobs had been made more secure by Eleanor Roosevelt's press conferences, prodded and criticized Bess Truman, but she refused to speak to them. One despairing reporter asked, "Mrs. Truman, how are we ever going to get to know you?" Bess replied, "You don't kneed to know me. I'm only the president's wife and the mother of his daughter." Thereafter, Bess held no press conferences. She did, however, maintain some contact with the Washington women's press corps. She assigned Edith Helm and Reathel Odum the job of conducting monthly press briefings. Beginning in October 1945, mimeographed lists of Mrs. Truman's social engagements were passed out to reporters. The lists were coordinated with the office of the president's press secretary. This effort marked the first time in the history of the White House that the East Wing and the West Wing worked together. Helm and Odum met with the women's press corps once a month, on Tuesdays, in the Green Room of the White House.[16] *New York Times* correspondent Bess Furman, a member of the women's press corps and an astute observer of Mrs. Truman, wrote: "It was not that Bess Truman shrank from holding press conferences such as those held by her immediate predecessor, Eleanor Roosevelt. She simply stood out like a solid wall against any such direct question-and-answer dealings between her and a public which she regards as wholly her husband's."[17]

Bess Truman finally agreed to answer a series of written questions in 1947. Her written, penciled replies were read aloud to the women reporters by Helm and Odum. The text was published in *Newsweek,* and portions of it reveal that Mrs. Truman was careful and at times evasive with her answers:

Q. What is Mrs. Truman's conception of the role of First Lady?
A. No comment.
Q. What qualities innate or acquired does she think would be the greatest asset for the wife of a President?
A. Good health and a well-developed sense of humor.
Q. Does she follow domestic and international events closely?
A. Yes, she does. Both.
Q. Does unfavorable criticism of the President disturb her?
A. After 25 years in politics she has learned to accept it to a certain extent.
Q. How would you add up what being First Lady has meant to you?
A. No comment.
Q. If you had a son, would you try to bring him up to be President of the United States?
A. No.
Q. Has living in the White House changed any of your views on politics and people? If so, how?
A. No comment.[18]

In private, Bess expressed her dislike of even the written questions. After one reporter's inquiry, she wrote to Reathel Odum, "Better tell her. God only knows what they might be saying. I'd prefer telling her it's none of their d—— business." When she reacted the same way to written questions about a gown she planned to wear, Odum sanitized it; she told the reporters, "Mrs. Truman hasn't quite made up her mind."[19]

Bess Truman's instincts were better put to use on matters concerning the West Wing press. She dismissed rumors that the *Kansas City Star*'s Washington correspondent, Duke Shoop, who had written a number of uncomplimentary stories about the Trumans, was to be appointed the president's press secretary. Bess wrote Mary Paxton Keeley: "He's made an ass of himself the way he broadcast the fact that he was going to be H's Press Sec'y. Even went down to the Press Club & spread it there of all places. If there is anybody on earth that H. has absolutely no use for it's D.S." Mrs. Truman instead urged her husband to appoint their Independence schoolmate, Washington editor of the *St. Louis Post-Dispatch* Charlie Ross. President Truman made the appointment.[20]

In spite of her rocky relations with the women's press corps, Mrs. Truman cultivated cordial social relations with their organizations. She and President Truman always attended the annual dinner of the Women's National Press Club held at the Mayflower Hotel. In February 1949, they were guests of honor at the American Newspaper Women's Club Ball.[21] And Bess Truman attended several luncheons held in her honor by both groups. She became an honorary member of the American Newspaper Women's Club in May 1945, during a luncheon held for the first lady at the Statler Hotel. Over one hundred members were present for the occasion. Mildred Kahler Geare, staff correspondent for the *Baltimore News-Post,* a member of the club, reported that Bess "made no speech, merely saying a simple 'thank you' for the lovely orchid which the club's president presented to her. . . . In talking with Mrs. Truman she made each one feel as though she took a personal interest in the conversation. She is one of the nicest, most charming women in public life I have ever met."[22]

Although reserved in public, Bess Truman had a good-natured personality and a winning manner. She also had a sharp, dry sense of humor. Guests at the White House learned that she had a remarkable memory. She seldom failed to get a name straight, and she paid careful attention to details that mark a good hostess. For example, she once sent a note down the head table to President Truman to remind him that the shy dinner partner he was ignoring was Dr. Lise Meitner, a noted atomic scientist.[23] Because of her reserved personality, Mrs. Truman remained a stranger to many White House guests, but they all respected her. She was never discourteous. "Her aloofness seems to be a matter of inborn attitude than of intent," observed Bess Furman. "It is impossible for Bess Truman to be anything but Bess Truman, who didn't give a hoot for the whole goldfish-bowl business."[24]

Mrs. Truman was one of the most modest of all first ladies. When *Call Me Madam,* a musical based on the life of the celebrated Washington hostess Perle Mesta, a friend of the Trumans, was produced on Broadway in 1950, Mrs. Mesta and Mrs. Truman went to see it. They arrived at the theater unannounced and stood in line for their tickets. An usher recognized Mrs. Truman and tried to escort her ahead of the other customers. Bess thanked him, but said firmly, "We'll wait our turn." As they entered the theater and walked down the aisle to their seats, the audience began to clap. The applause continued after they were seated, so Perle Mesta stood up and took a bow. Still the applause went on. Embarrassed, Bess urged, "Stand up, Perle. They want you again."[25]

Of all who came to know Bess Truman as first lady, the White House staff held her in the highest regard. Reathel Odum remembered, "Mrs. Truman was a most considerate boss. Although she was a no-nonsense type of woman, she was fun to be with and our relationship was pleasant. . . . We shared a small office together, and were on good terms with each other. I was never treated as a second-class employee by any of the president's staff."[26] J. B. West recalled, "There was little glamour to Bess Truman. Like most Midwestern women I'd known, her values went deeper than cosmetics and color schemes. She was matronly and comfortable."[27] Mrs. Truman had a genuine interest in each member of the White House staff and treated them with respect. To extend her appreciation, in 1947 she initiated White House "help weeks" that provided each member of the staff two free meals during their workdays. Most staffers had breakfast and lunch at the White House. Those who worked at supper time were offered a buffet of leftovers from the family meals. Head housekeeper Mabel Walker presented the weekly "help menus" to Mrs. Truman for her approval.[28]

Bess Truman ran the White House as she ran her own home; she attended personally to details that many of her predecessors had left to the White House staff. She also took charge of the bookkeeping and carefully watched expenses. When President Truman was interviewed by Marianne Means in 1963, he noted that an important contribution to his years in the White House was Mrs. Truman's constant effort to maintain the same kind of private, comfortable life they had shared before he became president. Bess rode to her old beauty shop in her chauffeured limousine and continued to pay only $3 for her weekly manicure, shampoo, and set because she "saw no reason to change." She continued to address her own Christmas cards; she played ping-pong in the White House basement with Margaret; and she hired housekeeper Walker primarily on the recommendation that "she keeps her mouth shut." Harry Truman recalled: "We never let anybody up on the second floor, where our private living quarters were, except our closest friends. . . . One of the biggest contributions she made was to see that the feminine part of the White House was run properly."[29]

In early May 1945, Mrs. Truman began a full daily schedule as first lady. She was an early riser like her husband. At eight o'clock each morning, she sat down for breakfast with the president and Margaret. At nine o'clock, Mabel Walker would bring all menus to Bess's desk for her approval. Sometimes she would pencil in changes on a menu. Afterward, she held household meetings in her small office. By late morning, she would meet with Edith Helm and go over her invitations, deciding which ones she could accept. Mrs. Truman also informed Mrs. Helm on what days White House luncheons and teas would be held, and when state dinners and receptions were ideally scheduled. Before noon, she would spend time handling her mail. At noon, if she was not attending a women's luncheon, she would lunch with the president. Early in the afternoon, she returned to work again on her mail. By two or three, she made public appearances or greeted visiting groups. She averaged two or three engagements outside the White House every day.[30] All her conferences were at her desk, and all her visitors were received in her sitting room. Bess retained one childhood passion: she remained an avid baseball fan. She went to see every Washington Senators game that she could fit into her schedule, and she listened to night games on the radio in her sitting room.[31]

Mrs. Truman earned the reputation of being one of the most socially active of all the first ladies. During her seven years in the White House, she attended 200 teas, 112 luncheons, 140 receptions, and 30 state dinners.[32] In the fall of 1946, she reestablished the formal White House social season, which had been interrupted by World War II, and personally directed the detailed planning of all social events, from formal state receptions to teas and musicales. "All over Washington," said Edith Helm, "I heard from people—many of them no friends of the Truman administration or its ways—nothing but praise of Mrs. Truman, her dignity and her unfailing cordiality when hostess at the White House."[33]

Mrs. Truman's schedule increased 50 percent by 1949. A sampling of a two-week span in the spring of 1949 shows thirteen engagements for her. They included a Congressional Club breakfast; lunch with the Senate ladies on Capitol Hill; a reception given by the White House aides at Anderson House; a reception for a branch of the American Association of University Women; a musical luncheon given by the Democratic Women's National Council; a women's luncheon of the U.S. Chamber of Commerce; a benefit tea for the Goodwill Guild of Washington; a luncheon with the 74th Club, an organization of the wives of congressmen who entered the House of Representatives in the 74th Congress; a handshaking event with a group of Home Demonstration agents from Vermont; and a reception for the Society of Sponsors of the U.S. Navy. Mrs. Truman also opened the Annual Flower Mart on the Pilgrim Steps of Washington Cathedral and attended the Washington Thrift Shop's white elephant sale.[34]

One of the first events Bess Truman hosted at the White House was a picnic luncheon organized by the ladies of the Truman Cabinet for the Senate Ladies Luncheon Club. Eleanor Roosevelt and the ladies of the Roosevelt Cabinet had originated the luncheons, and Mrs. Truman continued them through 1952. As a former Senate lady, she was delighted to serve as hostess and maintain contact with many of her friends. The expense for each luncheon was divided on a prorated basis, with each Cabinet lady contributing her share. Menus were first submitted to Mrs. Truman, and she then sent them to the Cabinet ladies for their approval. After late 1948, when the White House was closed for renovation, the picnic luncheons were held at the Blair House, and Bess Truman used the patio garden behind the house to seat the ladies at tables.[35]

The Trumans threw themselves into the job of entertaining official Washington. In early fall 1946, Mrs. Helm and Miss Odum called a press conference to announce that the formal social season, Thanksgiving to Lent, would open again. The White House agenda was made up of six official dinners for one hundred guests each, two honoring the diplomatic corps, and one each for the President's Cabinet, the chief justice and the Supreme Court, the president pro tempore of the Senate (since there was no vice president), and the Speaker of the House. The Trumans also announced five evening receptions: military, judiciary, diplomatic, congressional, and departmental.[36]

The receptions marked the peak of official entertaining, and they were spectacular. To make it easy for the Trumans to receive the tremendous numbers of guests, lines marched four abreast through the East Room. The receptions opened with elaborate formality. As Cabinet members and their wives arrived, they were shown to the president's study on the family floor of the White House. President and Mrs. Truman joined them there. At 8:45 P.M., fifteen minutes before a reception, four servicemen reported to a military aide in the main corridor near the foot of the stairway. Marching two abreast, they followed the aide upstairs and into the president's study, where the president sat at his desk flanked by two flags, the flag of the United States and the president's own flag. The aide approached the president, saluted, and asked permission to remove the colors. Two of the servicemen removed the colors, marched down the stairs, and took up stations to the right and left of the door leading from the corridor of the White House to the Blue Room.[37]

Precisely at the stroke of nine o'clock, the ceremony known as the Little Procession began with the president and Mrs. Truman descending the stairway, followed by the Cabinet members and their wives. The entire group proceeded through the guarded door. President and Mrs. Truman made their way to the handshaking stand under the chandelier in the Blue Room, and the Cabinet proceeded to less formal positions in the Red Room. At the conclusion of the reception, the colors were carried back up the stairs, and president and Mrs. Truman returned upstairs via the White House elevator.[38]

When heads of state visited the Truman White House, they were greeted with great formality. State dinners held in the State Dining Room usually took place the evening after their arrival in Washington. Mrs. Truman always approved the menus for state dinners and planned most of the details. Before dinner, guests milled about in the East Room, sipping cocktails or champagne as they waited for the presidential party to appear so the receiving line could begin. Only after going through the receiving line could the diners take their places at the table. Dinners were held around a large, U-shaped table elegantly decorated with arrangements of Bess Truman's favorite flower: talisman roses. During the winter, the first lady ordered the White House fireplaces opened and lit, and their warmth added to the festivities.[39]

World leaders whom Mrs. Truman entertained included Winston Churchill and his wife, Charles de Gaulle, Princess Elizabeth of Great Britain and the Duke of Edinburgh, Crown Prince Olav and Crown Princess Martha of Norway, Queen Juliana of the Netherlands and her husband, Prince Bernhard, the shah of Iran, the president of Chile, the president of Mexico, the prime minister of India, the prime minister of South Africa, the president of Cuba, the president of Brazil, and the governor-general of Canada, to name a few.[40]

Bess Truman wore elegant evening gowns for state occasions. Her favorite gowns had fitted bodices and wide crinoline skirts. All of them were designed by Madame Agasta of Washington, a fiery Italian whose sweeping gestures could trace Mrs. Truman's choices with talking hands. Madame Agasta would say, "She have taste. She never forget she is first lady." Bess frequently wore blue gowns, which accentuated her light blue eyes, including a light blue brocade gown that she wore for the 1951 state dinner honoring Princess Elizabeth of Great Britain. But there were variations from blue gowns. For a dinner honoring the prince regent of Belgium in 1948, Bess selected a pink crepe A-line gown. And in 1952, she donned a black taffeta gown with a beaded bodice for a second state dinner honoring Winston Churchill.[41]

In addition to thirty state occasions for heads of state, the Trumans hosted several official dinners during their administration: a dinner honoring General Dwight D. Eisenhower in June 1945; a dinner honoring all North Atlantic Treaty Organization Pact signers in April 1949; a dinner honoring the foreign ministers of American states in April 1951; and dinners honoring the vice president, chief justice, and Speaker of the House.[42]

Mrs. Truman worked hard at the job of White House hostess, making gracious conversation with guests. She also received countless groups of visitors to the White House. According to Jane Lingo, a school friend of Margaret Truman, Mrs. Truman wore one size larger glove when she left Washington because of shaking so many hands.[43] The visitors' list grew each year as Bess accepted growing numbers of requests for a reception with the first lady. By 1950, she was receiving over a hundred groups of visitors. They included the Society of Sponsors of the U.S. Navy, the members of the board of directors of the General Federation of Women's Clubs, wives of the officers of the American Dental Association, and the volunteer area administrators and field consultants of the American Red Cross. In addition, Mrs. Truman led tours of the White House for World War II veterans who were hospitalized in Washington-area hospitals. These White House tours began in early May 1945, but they ended a year later when the White House underwent repairs during the summer of 1946.[44]

Bess learned to enjoy the social functions for White House visitors and dignitaries, but humanitarian activities were much more gratifying to her. In January 1951, she postponed the teas that she customarily held for the wives of members of Congress and other officials of the government, and initiated a series of teas for Korean War servicemen who were hospitalized in the Washington area. The teas were held on Tuesdays and Thursdays from 4:30 to 6:00 P.M., and they became quite popular with the Korean War veterans. The first lady liked meeting the servicemen, and she continued the teas through the end of her husband's administration. Red Cross volunteers brought the veterans to the White House from seven Washington hospitals, including Walter Reed Hospital, the army and navy medical centers, Quantico Hospital, and Bolling Field Hospital. Occasionally, President Truman would drop by to thank the servicemen and shake hands.[45]

Bess Truman also lent her name to scores of charitable, patriotic, and civic organizations that asked her to be an honorary member, patron, or sponsor. She held honorary membership in many organizations, including the American Newspaper Women's Club, the Daughters of Colonial Wars, the District of Columbia Chapter of the Red Cross Motor Club, the Women's National Farm and Garden

Association, and the United Nations Club. In addition, Bess maintained an active membership in the Business and Professional Women's Club of Independence, Missouri, and she was an active member of Washington's Chapter S of the PEO Sisterhood. She also served as honorary president of the Woman's National Democratic Club and as honorary president of the Girl Scouts.[46]

In April 1945, Mrs. Truman accepted the Girl Scouts' invitation to become their honorary president. She viewed the scouting experience for young girls as important for building self-reliance and initiative, and as honorary president she supported the organization's international postwar projects. Eleanor Roosevelt encouraged Bess to accept the position, which had been previously held by several first ladies. "As you know, the President's wife is always asked to be Honorary President of the Girl Scouts," wrote Mrs. Roosevelt. "I have been asked to act as Honorary Vice-President, and also that I send you a line about their letter to you asking you to serve."[47]

In 1945, the Girl Scouts of the USA was the nation's preeminent organization dedicated solely to girls. It had been established in 1912 by progressive visionary Juliette Gordon Low with the hope of providing "something for all the girls." The Girl Scouts national headquarters opened in Washington in June 1913 and the movement spread rapidly nationwide. By 1937, the organization's twenty-fifth anniversary, there were 441,964 Girls Scouts in America and 4,778 active troops in practically every section of the country.[48]

Lou Henry Hoover had been president of the Girl Scouts in the 1920s. As first lady, Hoover worked with her scouting colleagues to increase membership and helped democratize the scouting experience. She also led a major fund-raising campaign. In 1931, Hoover asked the Girl Scouts to take part in the activities of the President's Relief Committee for Unemployment. In response, a National Girl Scout Committee was formed, and Girl Scouts nationwide collected clothing and held benefits for which an article of clothing was the admission requirement. Entire groups of Girl Scouts also cooperated in making new clothes for the unemployed, from layettes for babies to knitted sweaters and dresses for women and girls.[49]

Eleanor Roosevelt made her first official appearance as first lady when she was the principal speaker of the Girl Scouts' twenty-first birthday celebration in 1933. Mrs. Roosevelt was a vocal advocate for the organization through the Great Depression. When World War II erupted, she endorsed the organization's effort to become more aligned with America's national defense programs. After the United States entered the war, the Girl Scouts became involved in a variety of different ways. Scouts who had shown interest and talent in arts and crafts formed into corps of occupational therapist aides to help hospitalized servicemen. Those who had been interested in health and safety volunteered as hospital aides and nutrition aides. Others shouldered rakes and hoes and helped Americans plant 22 million victory gardens.[50]

During the postwar years, scouting expanded its programs into the international arena. Bess Truman had great interest in the Girl Scouts' Clothes for Friendship project to collect clothing for children overseas. The first lady sent the organization a supportive message when the program was launched in late 1945. "I wish every leader, sponsor and Girl Scout success and satisfaction in this very worthwhile endeavor," Mrs. Truman wrote the president of the Girl Scouts.[51]

The organization's goal was one million garments made up of 100,000 kits of ten garments each for children under age fourteen residing in Europe and Asia. Shipping and distribution of the kits were handled by the American Friends Service Committee. The first kits were sent out in December 1945 to children in Austria, Hungary, Poland, Germany, China, and Japan.[52] Described as one of the most ambitious efforts of the Girl Scouts, the Clothes for Friendship project enlisted the support of over 58,000 troops throughout the United States. The average goal, to be completed by December 1948, was two kits of new or reconditioned clothing per troop. All garments had to be attractive as well as useful, so that children in war-ravaged Europe and Asia who had worn rags and hand-me-downs could experience the pleasure of having a full wardrobe in good condition.[53]

Bess followed the project's success closely. On 26 May 1946, she received a group of Washington Girl Scouts at the White House. They presented the first lady with a six-month report and showed her the kind of clothing they were making and sending. After their presentation, Mrs. Truman gave the group a tour of the White House.[54]

Mrs. Truman's support of scouting's international friendship projects stemmed from her own personal interest in volunteerism and charitable giving. In January 1950, she endorsed the Girl Scouts' newest international goodwill endeavor, Schoolmates Overseas, which provided schoolbags filled with school supplies for children overseas. Soon after the first lady learned of the project, she wrote the Girl Scout national president: "I am very glad to have learned of the international friendship project which the Girl Scouts of the United States of America will undertake this year. It is always a pleasure to endorse any project such as this which will create good will between the different countries and bridge any differences created by language and geographic situations."[55]

In 1949, Bess also threw her support behind the Girl Scouts' first annual boxed cookie sale. Girl Scouts were invited to the White House to present the first lady with a box of cookies, and photographs were taken of the occasion. The Washington Federation of Girl Scout Councils wrote Mrs. Truman in 1950, thanking her for her public support of the cookie fund-raising sale: "The picture, which you so graciously allowed us to take last year when the Scouts brought cookies to you, was such an attractive one that we feel a great deal of the success of the cookie sale was due to its publication and the interest it aroused." Each year thereafter, Bess met with a group of Girl Scouts at the White House to receive their first cookies of the year.[56]

Mrs. Truman managed to add some variety to her usual schedule. For example, starting in October 1945, she organized a Spanish-language class and invited wives of Cabinet members and ambassadors. Another participant was Mamie Eisenhower. Bess's interest in Spanish began when Harry Truman was a senator. She enrolled in a course conducted at Washington's Hotel Shoreham, and when Truman became president, she had the class transferred to the White House. Every Monday morning, the class met in the Green Room. The instructor was Ramon Ramos, a Cuban American and president of Washington's Pan American Club.[57]

A philanthropic association that Bess maintained throughout her first ladyship was regularly attending meetings of PEO Sisterhood. She belonged to Chapter S of PEO, Washington, D.C., and she had been a charter member of the chapter when it was organized in 1941.

At that time, the *PEO Record* carried a report of its organization as a Missouri chapter because its charter list was made up of residents of Washington who were originally from Missouri. Bess served two terms as her chapter's vice president. The first lady regularly was hostess to Chapter S in the White House. She also entertained her chapter on board the USS *Williamsburg,* the presidential yacht.[58]

Mrs. Truman was a devoted PEO Sisterhood member because she supported the organization's philanthropic and educational mission of promoting increased opportunities for women in higher education. Although she never had the opportunity to attend college, Bess was a big supporter of helping women attain a college education. PEO, one of the pioneer societies for women, was founded in 1869 as a college sorority at Iowa Wesleyan College. PEO members later voted to retain its English letters and its off-campus chapters, thus changing from a college group to a community group.[59]

At the time Bess Truman was a member of PEO Sisterhood, the organization was nationwide. When Mrs. Truman first joined in 1941, PEO had 71,711 members across the country. It maintained three educational philanthropies: the PEO Educational Fund, a revolving loan fund established in 1907 to lend money to women who needed it for education beyond high school; Cottey Junior College for Women, a fully accredited liberal arts college in Nevada, Missouri, owned and supported by the PEO Sisterhood since 1927; and the International Peace Scholarship Fund, established in 1949 to provide scholarships for international students to pursue graduate study in the United States and Canada.[60]

Mrs. Truman made news from April through July 1946 when she invited the ladies from her Independence bridge club to spend four days at the White House. For twenty-five years, the Tuesday Bridge Club of Independence had been gathering twice a month for lunch and stakeless bridge. But never in its long career had it ever enjoyed a meeting like the one Bess had arranged.

During their stay in early April, ten members of the Tuesday Bridge Club ate in the State Dining Room, had high tea at the Blair House, sat in the presidential box at Constitution Hall for a concert, visited the Oval Office, and attended a Shrine Circus—and some even slept in Lincoln's bed. For several months after their visit, the press played up Bess's connection to her hometown, as in a July 1946

Life magazine article entitled "Bess Truman and Her Town," with a byline that read: "Washington is a dull place compared to Independence, Mo."[61]

When the house party in Washington broke up, the bridge club left for Missouri in four separate groups. Upon arrival, many were interviewed by the *Independence Examiner* and the *Kansas City Star*. A year earlier, members of the club had been interviewed on how Bess Truman would handle the job of White House hostess. After their stay at the White House, they found their unanimous prediction—that "she handles any job she undertakes, well"—was more than true. One member of the club declared: "Mrs. Truman has personalized the living quarters of the big mansion without detracting from any of its historic background. It has the atmosphere of a typical American family home." Others mentioned chance chats with members of the White House staff who spoke of Bess Truman's efficiency as a homemaker and of her kindness and consideration.[62]

Well into her second year as first lady, Mrs. Truman seemed to have developed a comfortable acceptance of her duties as presidential spouse. Her small East Wing staff operated according to her wishes, and the mansion ran smoothly under the guidance of J. B. West. In spite of her busy schedule, she managed to find the time to attend her Spanish class, entertain her bridge club for several days, and escape Washington in the summers to spend several weeks in Independence.

Whether Bess was in Washington or Independence, she always preferred to operate behind the scenes. Although she was a discreet first lady, she was efficient and hardworking. Many people were surprised that she remembered the names of their family members and details about their lives after a single meeting. She was so down-to-earth that they had to remind themselves who she was.

Bess Truman's genuine interest in others and her sense of humor made her a very successful White House hostess. The great many receptions, dinners, and teas that she graciously presided over and helped plan were a testament to her determination to make sure the Truman White House was a warm, inviting place to visit. Her willingness to serve as honorary president of the Girl Scouts and her active membership in organizations such as PEO Sisterhood were evidence that she, like many middle-American women in the 1940s and

1950s, believed that playing a key role in women's organizations would aid the development of a feminist conscience.

In 1955, Mrs. Truman was asked by Washington's *This Week* magazine whether she missed the White House. "I miss certain aspects of my job as First Lady," she replied. "It was a challenging, intensely interesting position, and I rather enjoyed tackling its many problems. The most tiresome of all tasks were the big receptions. I don't miss them one bit."[63]

Even though she never wanted to be first lady, Bess Truman adapted to her position. She had admired Eleanor Roosevelt, but she quickly realized that she had to redefine the role of being a president's wife to suit her own strengths. By projecting a homey public image and making sure her hat was on straight, Bess managed the White House social calendar with genteel grace and poise—but she also made it clear that her private life was her own business.

CHAPTER 3

THE WHISTLE-STOP CAMPAIGN AND AFTER

Bess Truman's intense involvement in the fate of her husband's presidency and her eagerness to push for causes she admired are evident in both her role in the 1948 election and her effort to get more women in government once Harry had been elected in his own right. Although her participation in the whistle-stop tours of fall 1948 is alluded to in accounts of that pivotal election, the extent of her commitment to the president's election is more far-reaching than previously known. Similarly, her drive to have more women hold appointed positions in government has not been much discussed in the evaluation of her contributions as first lady.

Bess Truman loved a good fight. She kept this side of herself carefully concealed, but it was the secret of her success as a tennis and baseball player as a young woman. By the summer of 1946, Bess and her husband were worrying about the 1948 election. His aide, Clark Clifford, noted that Truman's "greatest ambition . . . was to get elected in his own right."[1] Earlier, Bess had wanted to go home, and Harry's bleak electoral chances reinforced her decision, but a January 1948 poll indicated that the president could win a full term, and this news changed her mind. If there was hope for reelection, she would stand by Harry's decision to run, and she would do everything she could to keep his morale high. If that meant a more visible role as first lady, she would do her part.

The upcoming campaign forced Bess to relax her efforts to fight publicity. In the fall of 1947, she decided to cancel formal dinners at the White House because of the European food emergency, but she planned to host more receptions. During the 1947–1948 social season, the Trumans entertained 31,335 people in groups as small as 20 and as large as 1,500. They also accommodated 159,456 visitors to the White House in July and August. Aware of the widespread claims that she was frumpy, Bess also lost weight and changed her wardrobe, moving away from her practical gray tweed suits to more colorful ones in blue, green, and purple. She was steeling herself for another campaign. Her mother was in very poor health, but this time, Harry's needs took priority. Bess also asked Margaret to suspend her burgeoning singing career in order to prepare for a long fall campaign.[2]

Harry S. Truman needed all of Bess's political energy and talent in early fall 1948. He was waging an uphill campaign for the presidency that most of the nation's political pundits considered a waste of time. The Republican nominee, New York governor Thomas E. Dewey, seemed to be so far ahead in the polls that one of the nation's leading pollsters, Elmo Roper, announced in September that further polling was not worth the time and money. The latest Roper Poll showed Dewey leading by an "unbeatable" 44 to 31 percent.

Harry had been behind all year. Political leaders from William O'Dwyer in New York to James Roosevelt in California had publicly urged the president not to run. On the left, Henry Wallace, FDR's former vice president, led the Progressive Party on a platform that criticized Truman's policies toward the Soviet Union. On the right, Senator Strom Thurmond of South Carolina had taken the Dixiecrats out of the Democratic Party.[3] Confident of victory, ex-Republican congresswoman Claire Booth Luce gave a stirring speech at the Republican convention, announcing that Harry S. Truman was a "gone goose" and that Bess Truman was "the ersatz first lady who accidentally stumbled into the White House."[4]

Everyone seemed to believe that Thomas E. Dewey would win in 1948 except Harry S. Truman, Bess Truman, Margaret, and a loyal band of White House aides—and the small group of people who met the campaign train at Washington's Union Station on the morning of 17 September. Of that group, only Bess and Margaret needed no advance convincing of Truman's chances. They had seen Harry S. Truman win too many elections after the opposition had counted him out. But in 1948, the president had to first convince a majority of his White House staff, then the Democratic Party, and finally the American people that he was going to win the election.[5]

Someone on the staff intimated that there was no chance of winning; the best they could do was go down fighting. President Truman disagreed with that position. "We are going to win," he said. "I expect to travel all over the country and talk at every whistle-stop. We are going to be on the road most of the time from Labor Day to the end of the campaign. It's going to be tough on everybody, but that's the way it's got to be."[6]

Years later, aides maintained that Mrs. Truman played a role in coming up with the idea for a whistle-stop campaign. "If you ask me, the whole notion for the trip came from her," recalled Victor Messall, Truman's former Senate secretary who had become part of the presidential inner circle. "She would often tell Harry to run the way he did when he was campaigning for county judge."[7] Bess and Margaret also agreed to make regular appearances after Harry had given a speech. "Mrs. Truman and Margaret certainly stole the hearts of the people as we went along," noted aide William Bray.[8] Their appearance on the back of the train exhibited simplicity, honesty, and practicality. The three members of the Truman family sought to project the image of a typical American family.

President Truman also capitalized on the recent special session of the Republican 80th Congress, which had accomplished nothing. The Republicans railed against the idea of a special session, as a "last hysterical gasp of an expiring administration." Although Truman expected them to do nothing, he sent them a legislative package packed with badly needed bills on housing, inflation, civil rights, and aid to education. He asked them to increase the minimum wage, establish a meaningful national health program, extend Social Security coverage, and create a fund to bring cheap electricity to rural America. When the 80th Congress adjourned on 12 August, Truman was able to denounce their performance as a "do-nothing" session of a "do-nothing" Congress.[9]

The whistle-stop campaign traveled 31,700 miles in 33 days, and Truman gave 356 speeches—an average of 10 a day. There were four tours: first cross-country to California for fifteen days, then a six-day tour of the Midwest, next a tour of Florida and North Carolina, followed by a final ten days in the large population centers of the Northeast, culminating in a return trip to Missouri. Between 12 million and 15 million people turned out to hear him and cheer him on. No president in history had gone so far to gain support from the American people. Nor would any presidential candidate ever again conduct a campaign by railroad.[10]

The first family traveled on the *Ferdinand Magellan,* the private Pullman railroad car of the president of the United States. It had been purchased for Franklin Roosevelt's use during wartime. The windows were made of three-inch-thick bulletproof glass, and the whole car was sheathed in armor plate. For security purposes during the war, only the word "Pullman" appeared on the exterior, and in 1948, the only other distinguishing exterior features were three loudspeakers on top of the rear platform's roof and the presidential seal attached to the platform.[11]

The *Ferdinand Magellan* was very comfortable. At the forward end were servants' quarters, the galley, a pantry, and an oak-paneled dining room, which was also used as a conference room. Down an aisle were four staterooms, labeled A, B, C, and D. Stateroom C was the presidential suite with adjoining bath and shower. Stateroom B was the first lady's suite. In the rear was the observation lounge. The whole car was air-conditioned by an ice-cooling system, and each room had a telephone that could be hooked up to a trackside outlet. "Bess tried hard to make it liveable," noted Charlie Ross. "She saw that it was always clean and neat. But still she realized that it was only a railroad car."[12] The car directly in front of the *Ferdinand Magellan* was occupied by members of the Secret Service, and the fifteen other cars carried reporters, photographers, radio correspondents, White House staff, clerical staff, servants, and a few local VIPs who hopped aboard the train for short appearances before hometown audiences.[13]

The whistle-stop routine was constant. As they pulled into a station, high school bands would play "Hail to the Chief" and the "Missouri Waltz." President Truman, often accompanied by three or four local politicians, would step out onto the train's rear platform, and the people would present him a gift—a bucket of apples, ears of corn, homegrown peaches, or an item manufactured locally. Then one of the local politicians would introduce the president, and Truman would give a short fighting speech that plugged the local candidate and asked the people for their support.[14]

Whenever possible, President Truman would say something that he knew or felt personally. He told the crowd at Clarksburg, West Virginia: "I've always had a warm spot in my heart for Clarksburg. I have been a student of the War Between the States, and I remember that Stonewall Jackson was born here in Clarksburg." At Hammond, Indiana, where many World War II tanks had been produced, he spoke of the war effort. "Our armies all over the world were grateful for the high quality of work you turned out," he told his listeners.[15]

After approximately five minutes of praising the local candidate for Congress and talking about issues of local interest, Truman would lambaste the 80th Congress for the Taft-Hartley Act, for the high cost of living, and for cutting federal support for hydroelectric power and irrigation projects in the West. He also rarely failed to point out that they were a "do-nothing" Congress during the special session. Truman hit hard at Congress's failure to do anything about the housing shortage, and he frequently included himself in the problem. In Ogden, Utah, for example, he stated that if voters did the right thing on election day, "that will keep me from suffering from a housing shortage on January 20, 1949." In Colorado Springs, he told the people: "If you go out to the polls . . . and do your duty as you should, I won't have to worry about moving out of the White House; and you won't have to worry about what happens to the welfare of the West."[16]

"Give 'em hell, Harry!" someone would shout in the crowd, and others would take up the cry, followed by whoops and yells of approval—especially when he attacked the 80th Congress. At the end of each speech, amid loud hoorays, Truman would raise both hands, smile, and announce, "Here comes the boss." Bess would appear from behind the dark blue velvet curtains that covered the Pullman's back door. She would smile and wave in response to the noisy crowd, and take her place on his right side. Then the president would invariably say, "Now here's the one who bosses the boss." Margaret would join her mother and father. As the first family waved to the crowd, the train slowly pulled out of the station. Margaret later wrote, "We never did get him to stop introducing us this way in spite of numerous demands."[17]

By this time, President Truman was working with nothing more than an elaborate set of notes compiled by Mrs. Truman. Aides Clark Clifford, Charles S. Murphy, George Elsey, and Charlie Ross would write his speeches. Then Bess would carefully edit and outline them. Harry told her to omit any "two-dollar words" and to make the statement as simple and understandable as possible. She complied and helped him to speak effectively in his own Missouri way. When possible, Harry preferred to speak off-the-cuff. That was when his dry wit and sincerity came through.[18]

Bess sat in on most of the policy-making sessions and made recommendations that Harry often included in his speeches. In addition, she was a one-woman Gallup Poll, constantly testing the audience's reaction, keeping a sharp eye and ear on the crowds who listened to her husband's oratory. She would also carefully censor the president's occasional overexuberance, stopping attempts to throw his hat into the crowd or dance the "Missouri Waltz."[19]

In Shelbyville, Kentucky, reporters expected fireworks from Mrs. Truman when the president told a story of how his grandfather, Anderson Shippe, had run off with a local farm girl. The young lady's mother was so angry that she refused to sanction the union. Fearing the wrath of her parents, the couple moved to Missouri. Four years passed before there was a reconciliation. Truman said, "Confidentially, I've come to Shelbyville to see if my grandparents were ever legally married." The locals were delighted, but reporters were not sure Bess would approve. They were wrong. She smiled, shrugged her shoulders, and said, "Sometimes I just can't stop him."[20]

One thing Mrs. Truman did not like were the in-law jokes the president loved to tell. In Helper, Utah, the crowd roared when he compared the Republican Party to "big mouthed mother-in-laws who get all burnt up because they aren't invited to some kaffeeklatch," noting that Republicans were kept out because only the Democrats had a good relationship with farmers and blue-collar workers. "When Harry got back to his private car," Charlie Ross recalled, "Bess laid down the law to him. He never gave out with a mother-in-law joke again, but she never knew what to expect from him next."[21]

On 26 September, the Trumans stopped in Uvalde, Texas, to visit seventy-nine-year-old John Nance Garner, FDR's first vice president. Garner served them a typical Texas breakfast: fried chicken, white-wing dove, smoked ham, bacon, scrambled eggs, hot biscuits, peach preserves, coffee, and buttermilk. The large crowd that had gathered before dawn to watch them enter Garner's house was still there as they emerged hours later. Bess was so moved that she broke her public silence and said, "Good morning, and thank you for this wonderful greeting."[22]

From Texas, they headed to the East Coast states, making a preliminary tour of upstate New York on 8 October and cutting across the industrial belt from Albany to Buffalo before returning to New York City. During the New York City swing, Mrs. Truman received favorable coverage from the *New York Times*. At a stop in Yonkers, journalist Meyer Berger described her appearance: "Mrs. Truman, wearing mink and a blue bonnet with veil, smiled graciously and was warmly applauded. The women discussed her with eager animation."[23]

They ended the campaign swing in St. Louis. En route from New York, all of the speechwriters got together and pooled their best and brightest phrases for a speech they considered the campaign's masterpiece. Meanwhile, Harry took a long afternoon nap. When he woke up, the writers presented him with their tour de force, but the train was almost in St. Louis. Bess read through the speech, but she did not have enough time to write an outline. Instead, she encouraged Harry to give a completely extemporaneous address. He told his aides: "I'm sorry, boys, but I just haven't got time to get all this into my head." He threw the speech aside and walked out on the platform in St. Louis's Kiel Auditorium. Bess and his aides thought that he gave one of the greatest speeches of the campaign. The president concluded his speech by saying: "People are waking up. . . . and I'm here to tell you that if you do your duty. . . . we'll have a Government that'll be for your interests, that'll be for peace in the world, and for the welfare of all the people and not just a few." A reporter for the *Washington Post* told Bess that if the election was close and Truman won, he would credit the president's performance that night in Kiel Auditorium.[24]

The massive turnouts at each whistle-stop along the way encouraged Truman's supporters. Yet most newspapers and periodicals still predicted a solid Republican victory. The politically active left-wing support of Henry Wallace's Progressive Party was expected to take as many as five million votes from the Democrats. Southern Democrats predicted that Thurmond's Dixiecrats would have similar success below the Mason-Dixon Line. The final Gallup Poll in October, however, had showed evidence of a statistically tighter race, with Dewey at 49.5 percent, Truman at 44.5 percent, Wallace at 4 percent, and Thurmond at 2 percent.[25]

Their final destination was Independence, to their comfortable and much-loved house on North Delaware Street. Each of the Trumans voted on 2 November in Independence's Memorial Hall. Reporters asked the president for a final prediction, and he told them: "It can't be anything but a victory." Later that afternoon, he went to a lunch at the Rockwood Country Club, where he was the guest of honor at a party given by the mayor of Independence. After lunch, Truman excused himself. Followed by three Secret Service men, he went out the back door and drove to the Elms Hotel at Excelsior Springs, about twenty-five miles from Independence. There he had a Turkish bath, ate a ham sandwich, drank a glass of milk, and went to bed. Bess and Margaret were left alone to cope with throngs of frantic reporters, who surrounded the house on North Delaware Street. Bess finally talked Margaret into going out on the front porch to assure the crowd that her father was not in the house.[26]

President Truman later joined his campaign staff and friends from Independence at the Muehlebach Hotel in Kansas City at 6 A.M. At that time, he was two million votes ahead. Dewey finally conceded at 11:14 A.M. Truman won, with 24,105,812 votes to Dewey's 21,970,065. He captured 49.5 percent of the popular vote, along with 303 electoral votes, while Dewey won 45.1 percent and 189 electoral votes. When the word reached Independence, every siren, whistle, and automobile horn in town went off simultaneously.[27]

Bess was very pleased that Harry had pulled off a victory. She too had a few scores to settle with Republicans, primarily Congresswoman Clare Booth Luce, who had called her an ersatz first lady. The day after the victory, Bess came across a copy of *Time* magazine owned by Mrs. Luce's husband, Henry. On the cover was Thomas E. Dewey, described as the next president of the United States. "I wonder if Mrs. Luce thinks I'm real now," she said to Margaret.[28] "True to form, Clare was totally wrong," noted Charlie Ross. "Everyone who really knows Bess is very aware that she is solid 14-K."[29]

On 3 November, the Trumans left Independence to return to Washington. Their train was now called the "Victory Special." As it pulled into Union Station later that afternoon, Bess noticed that the crowd was enormous, but all she could think about was the loyal handful of supporters who had come down to see them off on the first campaign swing in September. Harry, at the urging of press photographers, happily held up a copy of the *Chicago Tribune* that bore the premature headline: "DEWEY DEFEATS TRUMAN." Bess usually tried to curb her husband's friskiness. But this time, she handed him the newspaper. The gesture was immortalized in what turned out to be one of the most famous photographs in American history.[30]

A few days after the election, Harry invited Bess and Margaret to travel with him to Key West, Florida, for a well-earned vacation. He had often escaped to Key West with staff and friends for a few days of relaxation and poker playing. Bess was exhausted after the whistle-stop campaign, and she eagerly accepted his invitation. They traveled south on the presidential yacht, the *Williamsburg,* in mid-November. Besides basking in the warm sunshine and swimming, Bess also enjoyed a day of deep-sea fishing. She and Margaret slept on the *Williamsburg* while the president and his male companions inhabited more Spartan quarters ashore, played poker and practical jokes on each other, and sipped whiskey. Near the end of their vacation, Bess and Margaret took a cruise aboard the *Williamsburg* to Cuba. They visited the Morro Castle, took time out for some shopping on the Prado, and had champagne with Señora Prio, Cuba's first lady, at the Presidential Palace.[31]

Bess did not realize how important the vacation was to her health until she returned to Washington. In early December, she traveled to Norfolk, Virginia, to present a silver service to the battleship *Missouri* on behalf of her native state. In the middle of the ceremony, she developed a severe nosebleed. Back in Washington, Dr. Wallace Graham, the White House physician, took her blood pressure and discovered it was extremely high. Dr. Graham immediately put the first lady on medication and a no-salt diet.[32]

During December 1948 and the first weeks of 1949, Mrs. Truman was more preoccupied by the health of her mother than by her own health. Her mother became seriously ill in December. Madge Gates Wallace was eighty-six, and Bess was so worried that she summoned her brother, Fred Wallace, from Denver. His presence helped Madge rally by Christmas. A few weeks later, Bess decided to move her mother to the White House. She wrote Mary Paxton Keeley, "We were afraid for a day or two Mother was not going to make it. But we got her back here [Washington] by air and she seemed no worse for the trip. And she can have every attention here and be under my eye too."[33] Thus, Madge Gates Wallace became the first mother-in-law of a president to live at the White House. Her move to Washington relieved Bess of making frequent trips to Independence. Madge remained with the Trumans until her death on 5 December 1952.

With her mother safely in Washington, Mrs. Truman shifted her attention to the inauguration. She spent the weeks leading up to 20 January 1949 bubbling with good humor and playing hostess to hordes of Wallace and Truman relatives and Missouri politicians. One thing that she certainly enjoyed was the large amount of money the inaugural committee had to spend. The 80th Congress, preparing for a Dewey victory, had appropriated $80,000 for the parade, receptions, and balls. For a frugal person like Bess, the inaugural turned out to be a spectacular celebration.[34]

Inaugural day was perfect; it was very cold, but bright winter sunlight poured down from a clear blue sky. It began at 7 A.M. with breakfast at the Mayflower Hotel for nearly a hundred former members of Battery D, which Truman had commanded during World War I. Bess and Margaret attended and watched as he was presented with a gold-headed cane. They told Bess: "We'd appreciate your seeing to it that the captain uses it on his early morning walks." She replied, "I'll see to it!" and remarked that the cane would last long enough for Truman to give it to his grandson. The president then gave the veterans marching orders for the parade. They would serve as the honor guard around his car on the ride from the Capitol down Pennsylvania Avenue.[35]

After breakfast, the Trumans attended services at St. John's Episcopal Church. Then they joined a joint congressional committee to escort them to the Capitol for the swearing-in ceremony. Margaret Truman later wrote: "As Dad raised his hand to take the solemn oath on the steps of the Capitol, I glanced at Mother and saw tears on her face. They were a mixture of joy and sadness. She still rejoiced in Dad's victory, but she knew that the next four years were not going to be easy."[36]

Mrs. Truman's dress for the inaugural ceremonies at the Capitol was designed by Madame Agasta, her Washington couturier. It was a tailored dress made of iridescent black and gray rajah pure silk with a slim skirt, but with voluminous lines at the bottom. It had a matching jacket with peplum folding into a pleat at the back. Her hat was made of Moonstone straw cloth draped with black nylon tulle and trimmed with a single pink rose.[37]

After a quick lunch, the Trumans participated in a long parade down Pennsylvania Avenue to the reviewing stand in front of the White House. Bess sat in the stand for three and a half hours. She applauded the Annapolis midshipmen, West Point cadets, scores of bands, and a team of Missouri mules. She thanked a delegation from Massachusetts when they presented her with a bouquet of roses. She waved at hundreds of people who made up the parade, but kept her arms folded when Strom Thurmond rode by with the South Carolina delegation. Instead, she turned to see actress Tallulah Bankhead loudly boo the racist governor.[38]

Bess left before the parade was over so that she could dress for a reception at the National Gallery of Art. A total of 5,628 invited guests attended the reception to hear President Truman and Vice President Alben Barkley give a speech. It was nearly impossible for Harry and Bess and Vice President Barkley to shake hands with everyone. Instead, a stand was built at one of the courts at the South Entrance, where they greeted over five hundred people.[39]

After the reception at the National Gallery, the Trumans prepared for a late dinner and the inaugural ball. Bess looked stunning in her inaugural ball gown, designed by Madame Pola of New York. It was made of black panne velvet and cut on slender lines, with the skirt draped to one side. The gown was floor length and slightly longer in the back. It was accented by a deep circular collar of velvet heavily encrusted with white Alençon lace, which fell gracefully over Mrs. Truman's shoulders. She also wore very long white kid gloves.[40]

The inaugural ball was held at the National Guard Armory. Ten thousand people crowded into the ballroom so closely together that they could only sway to the music of band leaders Benny Goodman,

Xavier Cugat, and Guy Lombardo. Because of the crowded conditions, Bess and Harry decided not to dance. Instead, they were content to enjoy the festivities sitting in the presidential box until the ball ended at 2:00 A.M.[41]

The inauguration ushered in a new beginning in Bess Truman's relations with the press. Reporters started celebrating her influence in private and her public grace, and they complained less about her reticence. In early 1949, the leading glossy periodicals profiled "The President's Boss," as *Look* put it. Bess personified genteel values: "dignity, reserve, conservatism." The "self-effacing First Lady" was "the same lady" she had always been, devoted to her family. *Look* also emphasized: "She doesn't try to save the world, nor to look like a Powers model. She's the very opposite of the brittle career woman."[42] After years of underestimating Bess, journalists suddenly pointed out her influence. She had become the president's secret weapon in 1948—influential behind the scenes and popular with the American people. A *McCall's* profile pointed out that the 1948 campaign, which had exemplified "simple American ideals," had been led by "a lady who stubbornly believes that the good life of a family need not be lost in the duties of a First Lady."[43] The 1949 portraits also kept Mrs. Truman's secret. Her father's death was noted, but there was no mention of suicide.

By 1949, both Democrats and Republicans wanted to restore the first lady's nonpartisan status. When a Senate investigation into Washington's "five per centers" and "influence peddlers" found that President Truman's military aide, Major General Harry Vaughan, gave Bess a freezer he had received from the Albert Verley Company, a perfume manufacturer in Chicago, the most partisan Republican in the Senate defended her. Joe McCarthy told his colleagues that the first lady accepted the freezer as she would a "twenty-pound cheese or a turkey." He added, "She just graciously accepted a gift and knew nothing of the background. She is the type of lady who is incapable of doing anything improper." McCarthy concluded that Mrs. Truman was one of the "finest things about the White House." The investigation continued into General Vaughan's activities, but throughout the session about these gifts, Mrs. Truman never spoke to a reporter or anyone else. It was beneath her to respond to smears. She was far more concerned about the terrible grilling General Vaughan took, and she backed President Truman's refusal to accept his resignation. Ironically, the freezer was a lemon. She had the Secret Service cart it away to the Independence dump.[44]

With the start of the new term, Margaret Truman moved to New York City to begin a singing career. Bess gave up her personal secretary, Reathel Odum, to be Margaret's chaperone. Living in Manhattan took the Independence out of Margaret's public image. In the meantime, Bess had overcome her doubts and encouraged the career. Most of all, she was glad to see her daughter get out of Washington. On 14 April 1949, Bess wrote Mary Paxton Keeley: "I am so glad you heard Marg sing and approved! Of course we are very proud of her—really, more because she had nerve enough to do it than of her performance. . . . Thank goodness she is really interested in something and is not content to sit around in Wash for the next two years—It becomes very deadly in a hurry."[45] Mrs. Truman had more time to devote to other matters with Margaret in New York City, and after the election she adopted a cause: the appointment of more women to posts in the new administration. In the postwar years, collective womanhood achieved its greatest unity pursuing the goal of expanding women's power by securing their appointment to government positions. A coalition grew out of a 1944 White House Conference on Women in Policy-making, organized by the National Federation of Business and Professional Women's Clubs (BPW), the General Federation of Women's Clubs, the American Association of University Women, and the National Education Association. The conference was attended by representatives of seventy-five women's organizations. It promoted women for both national and international positions. In addition, there was a less formal network of women in Washington who were active in other coalitions, many of whom worked in federal agencies. This group also worked with the Women's Division of the Democratic National Committee to lobby the White House for women appointees. Women themselves conceded that the results of these activities were not spectacular, but they were able to preserve the gains made by women during the Roosevelt administration, and they won a modest expansion of opportunities for women during the Truman administration. Mrs. Truman played an important role in securing more opportunities for women in federal government and she developed several contacts with these coalitions.[46]

As early as 1945, Bess Truman held White House teas for the General Federation of Women's Clubs and the Democratic Women's National Council, organizations that actively promoted women for national and international positions. Bess also attended several dinners hosted in Washington by the BPW, and she often invited the American Association of University Women to the White House for tea. Engaging with the women of these organizations allowed Mrs. Truman to learn more about their goals and provided opportunities for the women to communicate their concerns to the first lady.[47]

Bess Truman also attended, as did women appointees, a good number of parties and banquets sponsored by the Women's Division of the National Democratic Committee and the National Democratic Women's Club.[48] In October 1952, she hosted a tea at the White House for the National Democratic Women's Club to honor Eleanor Roosevelt.[49] During the parties and banquets, the women made many political speeches and were sometimes called on for advice on political problems developing within their home state Democratic committees.[50]

From 1945 to 1948, President Truman appointed only three women to posts requiring confirmation by the Senate. There were many women holdovers, however, from the Roosevelt administration who continued in office under him. The three women appointments Truman made during his first term in office were Eleanor Roosevelt, Frieda Hennock, and Frances Perkins.[51]

In November 1945, Truman asked Eleanor Roosevelt to be a delegate to the first United Nations general assembly in London. At first, she balked, saying she had no experience in world affairs. With Truman and others around her insisting, Mrs. Roosevelt soon realized that she had a duty to accept the nomination, knowing how much the United Nations meant to her late husband. She served as a delegate to the United Nations and as the universally respected and beloved "First Lady to the World," as President Truman first dubbed her, from 1946 to 1953. Her diplomatic skills were given recognition when she was elected chairman of the Human Rights Commission, a task that absorbed her energy and time for several years.[52]

Frieda Hennock, a New York City attorney, served as the first woman member of the Federal Communications Commission. Appointed in 1948, Hennock became an ardent proponent of educational television.[53]

Frances Perkins, secretary of labor under FDR, was appointed a member of the Civil Service Commission in 1946—something of a comedown for a former Cabinet secretary. Truman had refused to consider Perkins to head the Federal Security Administration, which was then under consideration for Cabinet status. Eban Ayers, the president's assistant press secretary, noted in his diary that Truman "did not want any women in the Cabinet." Bess was aware of his opposition to women Cabinet members, but she also knew that he was open to adding more women to top positions after his reelection.[54] As early as 1944, Truman had expressed his support of women's rights. With Bess's urging, he endorsed the Equal Rights Amendment while he was still a senator. "I am in sympathy for the equal rights amendment because I think it will improve the standard of living by setting a level of wages equal for both sexes," Truman wrote the Senate Judiciary Committee. "I have no fear of its effect on the home life of the American people." Six years later, the amendment passed in the Senate but failed in the House.[55]

In 1949, Truman was willing to consider a qualified woman for a top post, providing that the Cabinet members whose department was involved would agree. He was even willing, on occasion, to sell a potential woman appointee to a reluctant Cabinet member, as he did when he persuaded Secretary of State Dean Acheson to accept the appointment of Eugenie Anderson as ambassador to Denmark—the first woman to hold that rank.[56]

Many of the women appointees had the approval of Mrs. Truman, and she found a valuable and articulate ally in India Edwards, who had become the executive director of the Women's Division of the Democratic National Committee in 1948. Two years later, Edwards was elected vice chairman of the Democratic National Committee. Edwards modeled herself after Molly Dewson, the first director of the Women's Division, whose twelve years as the top woman in Democratic Party circles during the Roosevelt administration helped secure the appointment of over a hundred women during the early New Deal years.[57]

Like Dewson, Edwards kept a dossier of highly qualified women. She would routinely pore over the obituaries in Washington newspapers for vacancies in government posts. If a position had opened, Edwards would cull her list for a candidate, then contact Bess Truman for assistance. Mrs. Truman would review the candidate's credentials and would usually agree to counsel her husband to make the appointment. After she had the first lady's ear, Edwards would urge the president to consider a woman replacement.[58]

Years later, India Edwards gave Bess Truman credit for her advocacy on behalf of several women appointees:

> In many ways Bess Truman was an early advocate of female rights. She was instrumental in her husband appointing more women to top jobs than any previous president. There were nineteen women in key national posts and more than two hundred others as delegates, alternates or advisers to international conferences. Bess Truman earnestly believed that a woman is as good as a man—and she's the living proof.[59]

The top-level women appointees that had Bess Truman's approval included Anna Lord Strauss of New York City, who was appointed to President Truman's Commission on Internal Security and Individual Rights in 1951; Lucille Petry of Ohio, appointed in 1949 the first woman assistant surgeon general; Bernita Shelton Matthews, a Washington attorney, appointed judge, U.S. District Court for the District of Columbia in 1949; Georgia Lusk of New Mexico, appointed the first woman member of the War Claims Commission in 1949; Dr. Kathryn McHale of Indiana, appointed the only woman on the five-member Subversive Activities Control Board in 1950; Georgia Neese Clark of Kansas, a former bank president, appointed treasurer of the United States in 1949; Anna Rosenberg of New York, appointed the first woman assistant secretary of defense in 1950; Eugenie Anderson, appointed ambassador to Denmark in 1949; and Perle Mesta, appointed minister to Luxembourg in 1949.[60]

Credit for these appointments was given to India Edwards because she continually kept the women's cause before the first lady and the president. Mrs. Edwards was also the first woman to be offered the chairmanship of the Democratic National Committee. When William Boyle resigned in October 1951, Truman was willing to back her if she was interested, but she declined because she thought it was not yet time for a woman to become chairman. Bess always thought that India Edwards was the best candidate for chairman, but she respected her decision to decline the position.[61]

With Mrs. Truman behind him on the matter of women appointments, by the end of his administration, President Truman had appointed eighteen women to posts requiring Senate confirmation—one more than Roosevelt had named during his twelve years in office.

On occasion, Truman held fast when opposition was raised from powerful quarters. For example, he stood by Anna Rosenberg, a liberal Democrat, as assistant secretary of defense when her appointment was challenged because Senator Joseph McCarthy had spread the rumor that she was a Communist in order to defeat her confirmation by the Senate. Moreover, she was female and Jewish.[62]

At a time when McCarthyism was at its height, Truman's loyalty was an act of faith. His faith in Rosenberg was more than vindicated. She became the first civilian to receive the Medal of Freedom, which was awarded to her by President Dwight Eisenhower, and Secretary of State George C. Marshall was so impressed by her abilities to achieve consensus between opposing parties that he offered her the post of ambassador to Moscow.[63]

Bess Truman urged her husband to privately and publicly support his women appointees. They were prominently placed at the head tables at the Jefferson-Jackson Day dinners in Washington, displacing a few male Cabinet officials. Truman also inaugurated the custom of speaking by radio to women Democrats gathered at meetings throughout the country on Democratic Women's Day, and the president was joined in his broadcast by many of his women appointees.[64]

Bess also saw to it that Harry sent thank-you letters to his women appointees. He wrote Perle Mesta, minister to Luxembourg:

> I think you have done more to create good will for us in Occupied Germany, Luxembourg, Belgium and France than anyone who has been in any of those Posts since I have been President. Keep

> up the good work. It makes me feel very proud when people I appoint to office make good, as you have done.[65]

Mrs. Truman was also proud of the achievements of all the women appointees, and she hoped that by having them do their job properly it would set an example for other employers, which in turn would expand opportunities for women at all levels.

By the end of the 1948 election, the characteristics Mrs. Truman used as first lady were fully developed. During the whistle-stop campaign, she emerged as a savvy behind-the-scenes politician who projected a homey image. Because of her strengths as a campaigner, her relations with the national press improved. In fact, at the end of Truman's presidency "the Boss" had become more popular with the American people than Harry S. Truman himself.

In 1949, well into her fourth year as first lady, Bess Truman had proven that she was comfortable with her duties as presidential spouse. The East Wing ran smoothly, despite the loss of Reathel Odum, who had become Margaret's chaperone, and her social engagements and the social seasons were well managed by Edith Helm. For her special projects as first lady, she chose to focus on the appointment of more women to federal positions and on restoring the White House. With the help of India Edwards, she succeeded in persuading her husband to fill vacant posts with several more women appointees, and her great appreciation and respect of White House history guided her through four years of the mansion's restoration.

David W. Wallace. Courtesy of the Harry S. Truman Library.

Madge Gates Wallace. Courtesy of the Harry S. Truman Library.

Bessie Wallace at age four and a half. Courtesy of the Harry S. Truman Library.

Bessie Wallace (left) at sixteen with her lifelong friend, Mary Paxton. Courtesy of the Harry S. Truman Library.

Bessie Wallace and Harry S. Truman on a fishing trip in Missouri. Courtesy of the Harry S. Truman Library.

Harry and Bess on their wedding day, 28 June 1919. Courtesy of the Harry S. Truman Library.

Margaret and Bess Truman. Photograph by Vernon Galloway. Courtesy of the Harry S. Truman Library.

Mrs. Truman and others working for a USO fund drive. Photograph by Swann Studio. Courtesy of the Harry S. Truman Library.

Margaret and Bess Truman at the 1944 Democratic convention. Courtesy of the Harry S. Truman Library.

Harry S. Truman preparing to take oath of office in 1945 with Mrs. Truman at his side. National Park Service Photograph—Abbie Rowe. Courtesy of the Harry S. Truman Library.

The Trumans and the Snyders on White House grounds. Courtesy of the Harry S. Truman Library.

Indian chief and Mrs. Truman at the Congressional Club, Washington, D.C. Courtesy of the Harry S. Truman Library.

Mrs. Truman and Chief Justice Fred Vinson. National Park Service Photograph—Abbie Rowe. Courtesy of the Harry S. Truman Library.

Mrs. Truman at her desk in her sitting room in the White House. Courtesy of the Harry S. Truman Library.

Harry and Bess deep-sea fishing at Key West, Florida. Courtesy of the Harry S. Truman Library.

The Trumans visit the Kennedy White House in 1962. Photograph by Abbie Rowe. Courtesy of the John F. Kennedy Library.

And that's that! Leo Joseph Roche, Buffalo Courier-Express, *1956. Courtesy of the Harry S. Truman Library.*

CHAPTER 4

RENOVATING THE WHITE HOUSE

In the summer of 1947, President Truman made it known that he thought the White House's second-floor Oval Study above the Blue Room would be a better sitting room if it had a porch. Truman had various reasons for wanting to build what eventually would be called the Truman balcony on the South Portico of the White House. He wanted a place where he and his family could enjoy some outside breathing space with privacy. Bess Truman also disliked the ugly awnings that were used in the summer to shade the White House's downstairs rooms on the south side. The awnings were attached halfway up the mansion's beautiful columns and caught a great deal of dirt and grime. In addition, she informed the president that it cost $2,000 a year to try to keep them clean. When weather permitted, the Trumans took almost every meal under those awnings. Last, Truman said he thought the design of the building would be improved by a porch similar to those of old mansions in the South.[1]

When Truman announced his balcony plan to the Fine Arts Commission, who advised on and approved architectural plans for the nation's capital, the staid old committee protested, calling the proposed balcony "Truman's folly." The president reacted by saying, "The hell with them; I'm going to do it anyway." And he did.[2]

The Truman balcony was ready for use in the spring of 1948. Ironically, after all the protests and presidential determination, the balcony received very little use. "Mrs. Truman would sit out there every now and then," recalled J. B. West, "and they ate on the balcony a few times at night. But they found it to be too public for comfort. Crowds would gather at the end of the south lawn and gape at them as they sat there." Thus, the Trumans went back to eating on the South Portico, off the first floor, underneath their controversial balcony.[3]

Sparring about the Truman balcony was nothing compared to what followed. The Trumans soon noticed that the White House had begun to quiver and quake. In the winter of 1948, Bess held an afternoon reception for the Daughters of the American Revolution. She was receiving her guests in the Blue Room when suddenly she heard a strange tinkle of glass. Looking above her head, Bess saw the Blue Room's huge crystal chandelier swaying, clinking its hundreds of prisms back and forth. Still smiling, still greeting the ladies, she motioned to an aide and sent for J. B. West. "Would you please find out what in the world is going on upstairs?" she asked him.[4]

West hurried upstairs, trying to imagine what kind of scuffle was going on that would rattle the White House. He found the head butler stepping out of President Truman's bedroom. West, a heavy-set man, found when he retraced his steps across the bedroom, the floor creaked ominously. "This place has been squeaking like this for years," the head butler told West.[5]

As soon as the reception ended, Mrs. Truman joined West and the head butler, and they all stomped across the floor. "I was afraid the chandelier was going to come right down on top of all those people," Bess said. A few days later, the president's bathtub began to sink into the Red Room ceiling.[6] The White House, which had been under improvement with modern conveniences for nearly a hundred and fifty years, had chosen to collapse during the Truman administration.

The commissioner of public buildings, W. E. Reynolds, had a team of engineers run a stress test on the second-floor Oval Study. It was judged unsafe for more than fifteen people. An appropriation of $50,000 was made on 10 May 1948 to do a structural survey of the White House and come up with a plan to stabilize it. Meanwhile, as work progressed, a leg of the piano in Margaret Truman's room broke through two floorboards and knocked plaster from the ceiling of the family dining room below.[7]

As the engineers sifted through the White House, they found a huge split in a beam in the State Dining Room. In Margaret's sitting room, another beam was split badly. Many walls were cracked on the inside, and the floors sagged like a roller coaster's rails. The engineers also found no support for the interior walls, only soft clay footings.[8] They estimated that on those walls hung a weight of 180,000 pounds. Although the exterior sandstone walls, the roof, and a fire-resistant third floor that had been added in the 1920s, during the Coolidge era, were in stable condition, the rest of the mansion was on the verge of collapse. The entire second floor, most of which had been rebuilt after British soldiers burned the White House in 1814, was unsafe. "The character and extent of structural weakness were found to be truly appalling," said the commissioner of public buildings in his report.[9]

The Trumans met with engineers when they returned from the whistle-stop campaign. They were informed that the White House was in a dangerous condition and they would have to move out. President Truman replied to the group, "Doesn't that beat all! Here we've worked ourselves to death trying to stay in this jailhouse and they kick us out anyway!"[10]

The next problem was to find a place to live. Mrs. Truman ruled out the Blair House at first. "We need to keep it as a guest house," she said. "We've already invited six foreign visitors." President Truman then insisted that their new home be a government house. He had read about the criticism the Coolidges received when they moved into a private residence on Dupont Circle. The next day, Bess and Harry were taken on a tour of government houses. They settled on two choices, but circumstances gave them good reason to finally settle on the Blair House.[11]

One of their choices was the Peter Mansion, in Bethesda, Maryland, on the grounds of the National Institutes of Health. However, next door, a big construction project was going on—the beginnings of a large office building and hospital for the NIH. The noise and dirt would have been bothersome, Mrs. Truman noted. Plus, the Peter Mansion was a long commute to the White House. Their second choice, the Naval Commandant's house, on the grounds of the Naval Observatory on Massachusetts Avenue, would have been much closer to the White House. But the big frame house was not set up to accommodate the entourage that went with the presidency.[12]

So they looked at the Blair House again. It was suggested that the Blair House could be connected to the Blair-Lee House, next door, on all the floors. The Blair-Lee House was also owned by the government, and the two row houses together made one large residence. The Trumans finally agreed.[13]

The Blair House was one of the loveliest homes in Washington. Its scale, architecture, and furnishings reflected the best in nineteenth-century American design, and like the White House, it too had figured in American history. Built in 1824 by Dr. James Lovell, the first surgeon general, the house was sold in 1836 to Francis Preston Blair, whose descendants held the home for a century. It was Blair's daughter, Elizabeth, who married a grandson of Richard Henry Lee, for whom the Blair-Lee House next door was named.[14]

The Blairs not only entertained the presidents who lived across the street—Andrew Jackson, Martin Van Buren, Abraham Lincoln, William Howard Taft—but they also rented out the house to various Cabinet officials over the years. Henry Clay, John C. Calhoun, and Daniel Webster were frequent visitors. In 1942, the Blair House was sold to the State Department.[15]

The Blair House was exquisitely furnished with genuine period pieces, and Mrs. Truman had often remarked to her staff how comfortable the house had been during the first two weeks of the Truman administration. The Blair-Lee House, however, needed painting and new bathroom fixtures. "We didn't touch the furnishings in Blair House. But the adjoining annex, Blair-Lee House, was in pretty bad shape," recalled J. B. West. Carpenters, painters, plumbers, and electricians were brought in to renovate the Blair-Lee House, and doors were cut through on every floor, joining the two row houses together. After the painters had slapped on the last coat of paint, the White House staff moved the Green Room furniture into one room, the Red Room furniture into another, and the Private Dining Room furniture into the dining room. They also made a study for President Truman inside the front door. Bess and Harry moved in within two weeks. The White House staff and their equipment—china, silver, linen, and curtains—followed from across the street.[16]

President Truman went to Congress. Five months later, in April 1949, a law was passed establishing the Commission on the Renovation of the White House, with its six members appointed by Truman. The commission was made up of two members from the Senate, two from the House, the president of the American Society of Civil Engineers, and the president of the American Institute of Architects. Kenneth McKellar of Tennessee, the senior member of the commission and president pro tempore of the Senate, became chairman. Glen E. Edgerton, a retired major general from the office of the army chief of staff, was made executive director. But it was the White House architect, Lorenzo Winslow, who worked closely and directly with the Trumans, and it was the Trumans who made nearly all the major decisions.[17]

The commission presented three possible solutions: (1) to demolish the building, preserving and storing the exterior stones for later replacement, and to rebuild the White House from the ground up; (2) to demolish the building and erect a brand new White House, keeping the same design but building it of new material; and (3) to preserve in place the outer walls, to gut the interior completely, and then to rebuild it using original materials where possible, and exact reproductions where not.[18]

Bess Truman strongly favored the third suggestion. She thought that tearing down the White House would have been an act of desecration. President Truman also opposed the idea. "Most people think it was only Harry who had a deep sense of history," noted the secretary of the treasury, John Snyder. "It was also Bess. She took great pride in time-honored American institutions. Especially the White House. The country should be eternally grateful to her for the persuasive part she played in keeping it in one piece."[19]

Congress wanted to construct a brand new White House because it would be cheaper than trying to restore the mansion. That was when Bess decided that some lobbying was necessary. She buttonholed influential senators and representatives. "She pointed out that the public had long memories," said Snyder. "And that they would be forever angry if we abandoned the historic building." She telephoned wives of Washington power brokers who she thought might help, including Mrs. Robert Taft, whose husband, the senior senator from Ohio, was often referred to as Mr. Republican. "Browbeating was not her style," noted Mrs. Taft, "but she let it be known that the building had to be saved at all costs."[20]

Bess won her point. Ultimately Congress agreed to appropriate $5.4 million for the renovation of the White House. "It is the President's desire," Winslow wrote in the spring of 1949, "that this restoration be made so thoroughly complete that the structural condition and all principal and fixed architectural finishes will be permanent for many generations to come."[21]

The last major overhaul of the White House had been in 1902, during Theodore Roosevelt's presidency. Under the direction of Charles McKim of the renowned New York architectural firm of McKim, Mead & White, the main floor had been transformed from something resembling a Victorian hotel to Beaux Arts elegance, with the addition of new electrical light fixtures and chandeliers. McKim's work was primarily cosmetic, and it was done in a rush. Structural needs had been bypassed, making the White House less stable than it had been before. It had been truly a "botch job," as President Truman said, and McKim's work had been the principal cause of the conditions that the Trumans dealt with forty-seven years later.[22]

The interior of the White House had always been in a state of flux. The initial refurbishing came with Dolley Madison, who worked closely with Benjamin Latrobe to redecorate the public rooms. She created an image of the mansion that merged the populist sentiments of Democratic Republicans with the elitist tastes of Federalists. When the British army invaded Washington in 1814 and set the mansion ablaze, Mrs. Madison's scrupulous attention to detail was destroyed.[23] Later, James Monroe was the first president to initiate a redecoration project. Monroe had served as U.S. minister to France, Spain, and England, and his fondness for French decorative arts turned the house into a dignified and grand residence.[24]

President Martin Van Buren spent $20,000 that Congress appropriated for refurbishing his new home, following the wear and tear of Andrew Jackson's eight years in the White House. In contrast to Jackson's frontier heritage, New Yorker Van Buren's lifestyle was regal, and he saw to it that the mansion's redecoration produced elegance.[25]

Mary Todd Lincoln launched the next major refurbishing of the White House. Congress appropriated $20,000 for the Lincoln administration, but within a few months, Mrs. Lincoln had exhausted the sum. She ran up large bills by ordering extravagant replacement furniture, china, and window and wall treatments. An embarrassed President Lincoln wanted to pay for the purchases out of his private funds, but two more congressional appropriations finally covered the costs. Mrs. Lincoln's lavish tastes and efforts remade the mansion in classic Victorian style.[26]

President Ulysses S. Grant and his wife, Julia, completely refurbished the East Room in the bold New Grecian style that was popular during the Gilded Age. The next major refurbishing project came with President Chester Arthur. He spent $30,000 appropriated by Congress on redecorating the White House in the colorful style of Louis Tiffany. Caroline Harrison, wife of President Benjamin Harrison, collected pieces of White House porcelain used by previous administrations. Her collection culminated in the China Room display, which was inaugurated in 1917 under Woodrow Wilson's second wife, Edith.[27]

President Theodore Roosevelt and his wife, Edith, refurbished the mansion during the remodeling of 1902. They loved Victorian furniture, but they ultimately agreed to architect McKim's preference for Beaux Arts. Edith did insist that the Lincoln bed and other nineteenth-century furnishings be spared from the auction block.[28]

Grace Coolidge was known for her fashionable entertainment at the White House, but she also hoped to add historical furniture to the Executive Mansion. She began the "antiques movement" that Jacqueline Kennedy further developed in the early 1960s and that continues to influence today's White House acquisitions. Mrs. Coolidge encouraged donations of furniture from the early 1800s and created an advisory committee for decorating.[29]

President Herbert Hoover and his wife, Lou, loved Monroe and Lincoln furniture and memorabilia and collected them. Mrs. Hoover also subsidized, planned, and supervised the first cataloging of White House furnishings. Unlike the Hoovers, who were ardent students of White House history, Franklin and Eleanor Roosevelt considered decoration a mundane matter. Both had time-consuming public policy concerns during the Great Depression and World War II that overshadowed any refurbishing project. Mrs. Roosevelt did create an advisory committee for refurbishment of the Red Room and the Blue Room, but she ignored its advice when decorating the latter.[30]

The first dismantling began on 13 December 1949. The exterior remained intact, while within, everything below the third floor was removed piece by piece. Then came the full-scale demolition until the entire interior of the White House had become a cavernous empty shell. The old exterior walls were held in place by steel framing. Trucks and bulldozers came in to start excavation for two entirely new basement levels. "They took the insides out," Truman wrote in his diary. "Dug two basements, put in steel and concrete like you've never seen in the Empire State Building, Pentagon or anywhere else."[31]

The president, first lady, and Winslow worked well together. Winslow, a personable and gifted man, had been an important figure at the White House since the 1930s, and he cared deeply about the mansion. Winslow would write memoranda reporting on progress or detailing current problems, Bess and Harry would discuss them, and then the president would write his answers in the margins or between paragraphs in longhand.[32]

John McShain Inc. of Philadelphia was made general contractor. The firm had built the Jefferson Memorial and the Pentagon, and it had a high reputation in Washington. The Trumans approved of the firm's work, but when the president, walking over from the Blair House one morning, saw a large McShain sign on the North Lawn of the White House, he told the head usher, Howell Crim, to have "that thing" removed at once.[33]

For nearly a hundred fifty years, the outer walls of the White House had been standing on clay. During the restoration, for proper underpinning, four-foot-square pits were dug to a depth of twenty-five feet, down to a deep stratum of gravel. These some one hundred twenty-five pits were filled with reinforced concrete, thereby forming the foundation for the structural steel frame of the White House that was built within the original walls. The old brick of the interior bearing walls, which served as backing for the stone, were found to be too soft and had to be removed. When the bricks were chipped away, the inside surfaces of the original stone were revealed; many of them were marked with Masonic symbols.[34]

The original ornamental plaster cornices designed by James Hoban in 1792 were discovered in the East Room, hidden behind plaster put on in 1902. A well dug at the direction of Thomas Jefferson was found behind the east wall. In General Edgerton's temporary office on the South Lawn, an assortment of uncovered curiosities were kept: an ancient pair of workman's shoes, fishhooks, and a brick with the footprint of a dog in it.[35]

All the rooms of the main floor used for state occasions were to be rebuilt as faithful reproductions of the original rooms. The second and ground floors would also be restored with only minor changes. The best of original furnishings, those left behind in the move to the Blair House, had been put in storage at the National Gallery of Art. Mantelpieces, window sashes, old mahogany doors, and other hardware deemed worth saving for reuse, as well as all the paneling from the State Dining Rooms and the East Room, were numbered, tagged, and taken away to museums. The old bricks were taken to Mount Vernon for the restoration of garden walls.[36]

As the pace of demolition increased, a large quantity of material that might have been saved was discarded. Tons of scrap lumber, pine flooring and doors, old plumbing fixtures, and brick and stone were hauled away to landfills at Fort Belvoir and Fort Myer in Virginia. Door frames, plaster moldings (cast for reproduction), and chair rails were also scrapped. For over a month, dump trucks full of White House debris rolled back and forth across the Potomac to Virginia.[37] Before the renovation, there had been sixty-two rooms in the White House, twenty-six halls and corridors, and fourteen bathrooms. With the renovation complete, there were to be over a hundred rooms, forty halls and corridors, and nineteen bathrooms. In addition, there would be 412 doors, 147 windows, 29 fireplaces, and 3 elevators. There would also be a bomb shelter and a television broadcast room.[38]

Most of the additional rooms were on the third floor and in the new basement levels, which would resemble an up-to-date 1950s hotel. There were storage rooms, a medical clinic, a dental clinic, a laundry, a barbershop, a staff kitchen, and pantries. Very few buildings in America had such sophisticated electrical and mechanical equipment as went into the new White House. The central electrical control board filled a large room. Heating, air-conditioning, plumbing, elevators, kitchen appliances, and fire alarm systems—all were the most advanced of the day.[39]

To make the lowest basement bombproof, an additional $868,000 was spent. The decision to build a bomb shelter was made during the initial months of the Korean War, when many feared a third world war could come at any time. The addition of the bomb shelter required tons of additional concrete and steel in the walls and the floor above. It was completed in less than a year, long before the upstairs levels were finished.[40]

All work was to be completed by December 1951. In the early months, work had proceeded ahead of schedule. But with the onset of the Korean War, shortages of building materials became a problem and costs began to increase. The work continued six days a week. In the summer of 1951, the plasterers went on strike for several weeks, slowing progress even more. The laying of the fine parquet floors was particularly slow, because few craftsmen could be found who knew how the work should be done. The installation of marble and paneling was incomplete as well. Bath fixtures had yet to arrive, and even though twenty painters were at work in 1951, only the third floor had been painted. President Truman pressed for greater speed. He wanted to have at least one year in the new White House before his term of office expired.[41]

The contract for furnishing and decorating the White House went to B. Altman & Company of New York. The work was directed by B. Altman's young chief of design, Charles T. Haight. The increasing construction costs ruled out diverting additional funds for the purchase of early nineteenth-century furniture in Federal style. Instead, purchases were restricted to neoclassical reproductions of English and New England furniture made in Massachusetts by the Kaplan Furniture Company. Most of the 225 new pieces purchased were for the private quarters. Donations were offered, but the commission decided against adding to the historic "relics" already in the White House. It did accept several elegant late eighteenth-century English cut-glass chandeliers, a mahogany table in the Hepplewhite style for the State Dining Room, and a nineteenth-century clock.[42]

All changes in the rooms were approved by President and Mrs. Truman. Howell Crim, the White House chief usher, had assured Bess that she and the president would have the last word on the interior decorating on the second and third floors, and he made sure that they saw and approved all samples and sketches for the state rooms. Haight remembered that Mrs. Truman, and occasionally Margaret Truman, went over the drawings and inspected the samples. He gave them many alternatives and combinations, leaving Bess to make the final decision on the key fabrics used in the three parlors—the Blue Room, the Red Room, and the Green Room.[43]

On 15 March, the *New York Times* reported that things were "moving at the double quick" at the White House. "Two large moving vans stood under the White House front portico. From them movers carried furniture through the White House double doors. Graders were smoothing off a new front lawn just ahead of landscapers who were rolling down turf that arrived in great truckloads."[44]

Twelve days later, on 27 March, President Truman returned to Washington after a weeklong vacation in Key West, and, joined by Bess, he was driven to the White House, entering by the north gate on Pennsylvania Avenue. Beneath the North Portico stood the White House staff, members of the commission, and a small group of reporters and photographers. Along the sidewalk next to the iron fences, a crowd of onlookers gathered to welcome the Trumans back home.[45]

Because Bess had made a previous commitment to appear at a Salvation Army dinner at the Statler Hotel that evening, President Truman dined alone in the Family Dining Room, under a new antique cut-glass chandelier and a flawless replacement of the ceiling in which Margaret's piano had once poked a hole. "Bess and I looked over the East Room, Green Room, Blue Room, Red Room, and State Dining Room," he wrote that night. "They are lovely. So is the hall and state stairway. . . . I spent the evening going over the house. With all the trouble and worry, it is worth it." The renovation had cost $5,832,000, and he had been told by Winslow and the engineers that it had been built to last another five hundred years. He was extremely pleased.[46]

The following Sunday, a large gathering of press women assembled on the first-floor lobby of the East Wing. Bess Truman was to meet them on the remodeled second floor and show them through the family quarters. She appeared wearing a plain green two-piece suit. The tour was informal, and the newspaperwomen clustered around her. Pastel paints had given the wide halls and old high-ceiling walls an added feel of light and space and a decidedly modern accent.[47]

Mrs. Truman's southwest corner suite was composed of a lavender-gray bedroom and a pale gray sitting room. The walls of the president's bedroom were cream colored, his study off-white. All the other rooms had off-white walls, and all ceilings and woodwork were painted off-white as well, with the exception of Margaret Truman's northwest corner suite, where the walls and woodwork of its large sitting room were Wedgwood blue. Reporter Bess Furman noted, "The greatest marvel of all is Margaret's newly built-in corner closet with an mandarin-like top." The White House had always used wardrobes, and still used them in the president's bedroom and in all state guest rooms.[48]

In Margaret's sitting room was her own baby grand piano, a large library of records, a collection case filled with miniatures, settees and chairs grouped around a fireplace topped by a tall mirror in an elaborate gilded frame, and a beautiful dark red oriental rug. There was an ivory Hollywood bed instead of the prevailing four-poster colonial in her bedroom, decorated with sprigs of pink roses, with a dressing table and stool to match. Mrs. Truman's small bedroom was made homey by several photographs of her husband and one of Margaret as a child. An oil painting of President Truman also dominated Bess's sitting room. Flower prints were used in the decoration of both rooms.[49]

President Truman had the piano, which used to stand in one corner of the Monroe sitting room, moved into his Oval Study, so whenever he found time to break from work, he could ripple off a few notes. There was also a spinet piano at the end of the central hall, between Mrs. Truman's suite and Margaret's.[50]

President Truman retained the same bedroom and same study that President Roosevelt had. His desk was close to the windows overlooking the Washington Monument. His bed was a four-poster with blue silk canopy and crocheted spread. Nearby was a leather couch. His wardrobe was large and "mannish-looking" with a full-length mirror on its front.[51]

Adjoining the president's study on the east was the Monroe Room, which was furnished with the Monroe furniture reproductions previously used in the room, although restored, refinished, and reupholstered. The room was dominated by an eighteenth-century document print of fruits and flowers in rose and blue. With its desk, great breakfront bookcase, and miscellaneous sofas and lounge chairs, the room had a simple dignity suited to its historical background.[52]

In the Lincoln Bedroom, the great Victorian bed, some of the Lincoln cabinet chairs, his desk, a marble-topped table, and other items of furnishings belonging to Lincoln were used as a background of that period. The floor covering was a Brussels carpet of yellow roses and green leaves on a beige background. The room was painted yellow, above white dado and trim. The windows were curtained in embroidered batiste hung beneath valances of green taffeta. The bedspread was a white linen woolsey heavily fringed with cotton.[53] The Rose Room, across the hall from the Lincoln Bedroom, had been repainted a soft mauve. The eighteenth-century furniture reproductions previously used in the room were restored, refinished, and reupholstered in rose-colored velvet. The Rose Room had been occupied by Churchill in his numerous visits to the Truman White House.[54]

For all the rooms on the second floor except the Lincoln Bedroom, some museum prints of the Georgian period had been found and used as inspiration for the rest of the decoration. The one used in Mrs. Truman's sitting room off the West Hall was a floral print of amethyst-colored flowers and green leaves on an ivory background. The carpet there was amethyst-colored chenille.[55] Bess Truman and the press women climbed to the third floor and saw guest suite after suite with a small sitting room and bath. They also viewed the solarium overlooking the South Grounds and a new playroom for White House children and child visitors. Each of the rooms was smaller than the rooms of the second floor and was decorated in a more informal manner. Eighteenth-century reproductions of mahogany beds, chest, draperies, and other appurtenances were used, and some of the furniture pieces were reproductions of the famous Williamsburg Collection.[56]

As Bess led the press corps back to the main floor of the White House, inside the north door, they walked into the grand new entrance. The addition of cream-colored marble had transformed the entrance hall from a country house to postwar modernism. Joliet stone flooring pavers had been replaced by grayish white marble, and the column screen that had once been plaster was all marble.

Centered on the east wall was the opening to the revised grand stair, featuring a single range of stairs rising in several lengths. The bottom landing, where the president and first lady appeared, was wide and elevated so that dinner guests filling the hall could see them with ease. A new red chenille rug in the east–west portion of the hall extended from the east to the west rooms, and a set of walnut-framed Louis XVI benches had been added.[57]

Mrs. Truman then allowed the press women to meander through the main floor. Any visitor to the state rooms would not have noticed dramatic changes. Many of the furnishings had been returned to their previous locations. Little had changed in the Green Room. It had been completely redecorated and its old furnishings restored only a few months before the White House was vacated. The floor covering of the Green Room was a hand-tufted rug reproduced, including the President's Seal, from an old Aubusson rug that had originally covered the room. The walls and draperies were of bright emerald green silk damasks from the mid-1940s. The monotony of its color scheme was relieved by a love seat and two occasional chairs upholstered in a much lighter shade of green than the walls, rug, and armchairs. But the new, vivid colors of the wall coverings and upholsteries in the Blue Room and the Red Room reflected the postwar modern tastes of Mrs. Truman. The Blue Room walls, formerly a solid blue rep, were covered with a gold neoclassical floral design and blue silk satin. Its lovely parquetry floor was left bare, as in the old days. Hangings, too, were blue and gold, and the furniture white, blue, and gold. It was much livelier than the old Blue Room. The Red Room damask, copied from an eighteenth-century design, was a brilliant lipstick red, as was the red chenille carpet that covered the floor wall to wall. The only accent in the Red Room was white damask used on a set of open-arm Hepplewhite chairs and a handsome Chippendale wing chair.[58]

For the East Room, with its painted wood paneling, a white and lemon-gold silk damask had been woven from an old document characteristic of many used in the eighteenth century. The material was made into seven pairs of draperies with festooned valances hung beneath gilded cornices. Portraits of George and Martha Washington hung on the east wall of the room, and beneath was a pair of original Adam sofas. The sofas had been reupholstered blue, and they were the only blue accent in the otherwise gold and white room.[59]

The most dramatic change was in the State Dining Room, where the old English oak-paneled walls, which dated back to the Theodore Roosevelt remodeling, were painted celadon green. This decision, like all others dealing with changes in the state rooms, was approved by Mrs. Truman. The room was hung with red damask draperies. The Family Dining Room was also hung with the same red damask draperies. A large Sheraton sideboard and Hepplewhite table with a set of Chippendale chairs furnished the room. Of fourteen chandeliers that had been donated to the White House, the most beautiful went to the Family Dining Room, which had never had a chandelier.[60]

Mrs. Truman did not take the press women to the ground floor, where the principal rooms were the diplomatic reception room, the China Room, the old billiard room, and the library. Those rooms had been draped with fabric reused from the first floor of the old White House. A few old wing chairs and tables contributed to the furnishing of the library, and on the floor was the old Aubusson rug from the Green Room. In the old billiard room was the Lincoln cabinet table, a Victorian piece that had been expertly restored and recovered with a new leather top.[61]

A notable room of the ground-floor restoration was the original kitchen of the White House, with its vaulted ceilings and a stone fireplace at each end. It was replaced during the restoration with a new and modern kitchen, and the original was turned into a conference room and broadcasting room. Black leather sofas of 1950s vintage and reupholstered lounge chairs in handwoven English tapestry furnished the broadcasting room, together with an old pine table and a great hutch built from old rafters of the mansion at the time the building was reconstructed in 1815–1817. A silk and linen damask drapery covered the windows, and a coarse-textured hand-tufted rug covered the floor.[62]

The White House reopened for public tours on 22 April 1952, and a record-breaking 5,444 people went through. On 3 May, President Truman led his own televised tour of the mansion. All three networks carried the broadcast, and three network announcers—Walter Cronkite of CBS, Frank Bourgholtzer of NBC, and ABC's Bryson

Riash—took turns accompanying him and asking questions. Thirty million Americans watched the broadcast.[63]

Bess also watched her husband from a Blair House television. She thought he seemed gracious, relaxed, and knowledgeable. She was proud of the restoration. Moreover, she was pleased that the country loved the new White House. Her role in the redecoration had been significant. With their new paint, furniture, fabrics, and carpets, the renovated rooms had a fresh and clean appearance. Reporters commented on the "smartness" of interiors that had been "purified" in an authentic fashion. It no longer seemed like the old White House that had been part of a hundred fifty years of national life. Yet within the historic walls, it was prepared for the vast expansion of the presidency that had come with World War II and would continue in the last half of the twentieth century.

CHAPTER 5

PARTNER AND ADVISER

Bess Wallace Truman had a passion for anonymity that made her one of the least known first ladies. Yet she was also one of the most influential. Harry Truman frequently referred to her as his helper. "She was a full partner in all my transactions—politically and otherwise," said the former president in 1963. He consulted her about every important decision of his life, including some of the great crises of American history, such as whether to use the atomic bomb on Nagasaki, whether to initiate the Marshall Plan to rebuild a shattered Europe, and whether to fight in Korea. The final decision was always the president's alone, of course. But first, "I discussed all of them with her," Truman said. "Why not? Her judgment was always good. She never made a suggestion that wasn't for the welfare and benefit of the country and what I was trying to do."[1]

The Truman marriage was a productive working partnership. An important aspect of the partnership was no nagging. Bess would give her opinion on an issue. If Harry's opinion differed and he went in another direction, that was the end of the matter. She never waylaid him or tried to change his mind. Only when he hesitated between two difficult choices would she prod him to act one way or the other.[2]

Few presidents in American history have had to make world-shaping decisions faster than Harry S. Truman. Between 12 April, when he took the oath of office, and 2 September, he presided over the end of the war against Germany, oversaw the opening of the United Nations, and concluded the war with Japan. In these decisions and events, Bess Truman played little part. During these early months, she began to think that the presidency had almost dissolved the political partnership that had been at the center of her relationship with her husband for many years.[3]

Another partnership role Bess played was censor. Harry Truman had a quick temper. She did not think the president of the United States should tell others to go to hell or inform someone he was an SOB. Harry did not use profanity in his everyday speech. But when he became angry, his language could be salty. In the White House, it became a running joke among the staff whether the president "was in the doghouse again" for sounding off.[4]

Another partnership role, which Mrs. Truman shared with many other first ladies, was protector. Harry Truman had an enormous appetite for work. When a crisis erupted in the White House he would work until 3:00 or 4:00 A.M., driving himself and his staff to near-exhaustion. That was when Bess stepped in and said, "Harry, it's time for a vacation." He rarely demurred. In 1947, after frantic weeks of work to rescue Greece from a Communist takeover, when he finally retreated to his favorite hideaway in Key West, he wrote Margaret: "I had no idea I was so tired. I have been asleep most of the time. No one, even me, knew how worn to a frazzle the chief executive had become."[5]

The Trumans—Harry, Bess, and Margaret—depended on one another, and they were even nicknamed "the Three Musketeers" by the White House staff. But according to Margaret, even with her family, Bess remained emotionally unexpressive. Harry was the only one to whom Bess opened up. When he caught her burning letters she had written to him, he tried to stop her with a reminder to "think of history." As she threw the rest of the stack into the flames, she responded, "I am." Although she did not think her letters worthy of preservation, she preserved Harry's to her.[6] His "Dear Bess" letters have survived to serve as valuable sources, revealing exactly what Bess knew and when she knew it.

In mid-July 1945, President Truman traveled for three weeks to the Potsdam conference just outside Berlin. He noted in his diary that Bess "wasn't happy about my going to see Mr. Russia and Mr. Great Britain—neither am I." Instead of worrying about Joseph Stalin or Winston Churchill, the president worried about his wife. "I'm sorry if I've done something to make you unhappy," he wrote Bess. "All I've ever tried to do is make you pleased with me and the world. I'm very much afraid I've failed miserably." Whenever Harry feared he was in trouble with Bess, he searched for ways to prove he was worthy of her. Following a transatlantic phone call from Berlin to Independence, he confessed: "I spent the day . . . trying to think up reasons why I should bust up the conference and go home."[7]

To what extent President Truman consulted with the first lady about dropping the atomic bomb is uncertain. When questioned directly on it, he said he had. Margaret claimed that he had merely informed Bess. Mrs. Truman was in Missouri when the first bomb was detonated over Hiroshima, but she was back in Washington just before the second bomb was dropped. Evidently, the president did seek her advice on the latter, targeted on Nagasaki. The night before he issued the order, White House butler Charles Ficklin said the Trumans were in their nightly meeting upstairs in the president's study much longer than usual. When they emerged, "both looked real serious," said Ficklin. "Usually, they'd joke or kid around before going to bed. Now they didn't say a word, just looked straight ahead."[8]

Throughout 1945, Bess was often frustrated with Harry about his many absences. She insisted on spending Christmas in Independence, and the president kept postponing his plans to join her and Margaret. He finally flew through a sleet storm so severe that all commercial aircraft had been grounded, and he arrived just in time for Christmas. Bess, who disliked airplanes and was terrified for his safety, lambasted him, telling him he could have stayed in Washington for all she cared.[9]

Two days later, Harry had to fly back to Washington for a meeting with his secretary of state. The next day, 28 December, a despondent president wrote Bess:

> You can never appreciate what it means to come home as I did the other evening after doing at least one hundred things I didn't want to do and have the only person in the world whose approval and good opinion I value look at me like I'm something the cat

> dragged in and tell me I've come in at last because I couldn't find any reason to stay away. I wonder why we are made so that what we really think and feel we cover up?[10]

Harry could not cope with Bess's disapproval at that critical time. "You, Margie and everyone else who may have any influence on my actions must give me help and assistance. . . . If I can get the use of the best brains in the country and a little bit of help from those I have on a pedestal at home, the job will be done."[12] When Bess received the letter, the impasse between the Trumans ended. Margaret recalled that the first lady returned to Washington "in a much improved mood. . . . The air had been cleared of her smoldering resentment." Thereafter, Mrs. Truman played an increasing role as advisor to her husband.[11]

After Chief Justice Harlan Fiske Stone died in 1946, President Truman was able to nominate his replacement, and Mrs. Truman played an important role in the selection process, leading to the nomination of Fred M. Vinson.

Vinson had been elected to the U.S. House of Representatives from Kentucky in 1924. He was elected as a Democrat and was reelected twice before losing in 1928. However, he came back to win reelection in 1930, and he served in Congress through 1937. While in Congress, Vinson befriended Senator Truman. He soon became a close advisor, confidant, poker player, and dear friend. Bess was also fond of Vinson; she called him "Pap." Moreover, she was a close friend of Vinson's wife, Roberta.[12]

Bess advised Harry to choose Vinson as chief justice over several other candidates. Vinson had a judicial record that impressed her, and she thought that he had the temperament that would make an excellent chief justice. Vinson had been nominated by FDR in 1937 to the U.S. Court of Appeals for the District of Columbia circuit. While he was there, he was designated by Chief Justice Stone in 1942 as chief judge of the U.S. Emergency Court of Appeals. He resigned from the bench in 1943 to become director of the Office of Economic Stabilization. President Truman appointed Vinson secretary of the treasury, and Vinson oversaw the Treasury Department from 23 July 1945 to 23 June 1946. Vinson's mission as secretary of the treasury was to stabilize the American economy during the last months of World War II and to adapt the United States' financial position to the drastically changed circumstances of the postwar world. Before the war ended, he also directed the last of the great war-bond drives.[13]

Throughout much of May 1946, Harry leaned toward nominating his longtime friend. His decision was final when Bess gave her nod of approval. The Senate confirmed Vinson by a voice vote on 20 June. Two days later, Harry wrote Bess:

> I have fixed up a grand ceremony for Mr. Vinson. Going to do it on the south portico with all the trimmings—band, Supreme Court, ambassadors, Cabinet, Congress, and the common people. If that doesn't create some respect for the Court I know of nothing else to do. Anyway very few in my position have the chance to make a Chief Justice.[14]

Vinson took the oath of office as chief justice on 24 June, and during his time on the Court, he wrote seventy-seven opinions for the Court and thirteen dissents. His most dramatic dissent was when the Court voided President Truman's seizure of the steel industry during a strike in a 3 June 1952 decision, *Youngstown Sheet & Tube Co. v. Sawyer*. The Vinson Court also challenged the "separate but equal" decision of 1896 and paved the way for striking it down in 1954. The first important case involving civil rights was *Shelly v. Kraemer* (1948), in which Chief Justice Vinson declared that housing covenants "defined wholly in terms of race and color" violated the Fourteenth Amendment and therefore no court could enforce them. Other important civil rights cases were decided in 1950. In *Henderson v. U.S.*, the court declared that segregation of railroad dining cars was illegal under the Interstate Commerce Act. *McLaurin v. Oklahoma State Regents* forbade the separation of a black student from other students at the University of Oklahoma. And *Sweatt v. Painter*, under the Fourteenth Amendment, forbade a separate black law school in Texas. Vinson's final public appearance at the Court was when he read the decision not to review the conviction and death sentence of Julius and Ethel Rosenberg. He died unexpectedly from a heart attack on 8 September 1953.[15]

Bess Truman's second major role as advisor to her husband led to the forced resignation of the secretary of commerce, Henry Wallace, in September 1946. Mrs. Truman never liked or trusted Wallace because he represented the far left wing of the Democratic Party. She also thought that he was an inept politician. Wallace had served as FDR's secretary of agriculture, and the notion that he was President Roosevelt's successor had gone to his head. Bess believed that Wallace was uncompromising, and she noticed that he did not know how to fraternize. Her opinion of Wallace had run counter to that of Eleanor Roosevelt. In her newspaper column, "My Day," and among her friends, Mrs. Roosevelt backed Wallace enthusiastically. But in 1944, both the incumbent first lady and Bess Truman watched with interest as the Democratic convention beat off an attempt by Wallace supporters to stampede the delegates and instead nominated Harry S. Truman for vice president.[16]

When Truman became president, he made Wallace his secretary of commerce—one of two Rooseveltians in his Cabinet. As a Cabinet member, Wallace attempted to push Truman around. As matters turned out, Wallace's actions gave Bess Truman good reason to believe that he had intentionally embarrassed her husband, that he was no team player, and that he must be removed from the Cabinet.[17]

Wallace's departure was messy. The secretary of commerce came to see the president on 10 September 1946 to read a speech that he planned to give two days later at Madison Square Garden. President Truman read portions of the speech and believed everything was all right, although it dealt with policy toward Russia—a sensitive subject because the cold war was heating up. On the day of the speech, reporters received advance copies, and Truman took a question in his 4:00 P.M. press conference that asked whether he had approved of what Wallace was to say. Truman told reporters he approved. Later, the press secretary, Charlie Ross, called Truman to inform him that the State Department had received a copy of the speech and did not like it.[18]

At Madison Square Garden, Wallace, departing from his prepared text, told an audience of 20,000 that the United States had "no more business in the political affairs of Eastern Europe than Russia has in the political affairs of Latin America." Wallace concluded that any "get tough policy" was foolhardy. "The tougher we get, the tougher the Russians will get," Wallace emphasized. He also condemned

British "imperialism" and advocated American and Russian spheres of interest in the world, a policy strongly opposed by Secretary of State James Byrnes.[19]

At a press conference on 14 September, Truman admitted he had made a grave "blunder." There had been "a natural misunderstanding," Truman said. It had been his intention to express approval of Secretary Wallace's right to give the speech, not approve of the speech itself.[20]

The Wallace affair went on for several days. President Truman consulted with the first lady, and she thought that the only recourse was to fire Wallace. Harry took Bess's advice seriously, but he was reluctant to remove the last New Dealer in the Cabinet. Wallace was too important symbolically. The secretary of commerce and the president met again in the Oval Office on 18 September. By that time, Mrs. Truman had departed Washington for Independence. Wallace told the president that America's greatest issue was foreign policy, and he thought that he had to address it in his speeches. He also insisted that he wanted to remain in the Cabinet as Truman's "left hand," as spokesman of the left-wing group of Democrats. During the course of the resignation, no statement Wallace made hurt him more than the remark that he should be the president's left hand. Truman interpreted it as the end justifying the means. Wallace had to go. On 20 September, Truman sent Wallace a letter asking for his resignation.[21]

On 21 September, Harry informed Bess that he had fired Wallace:

> Well I fired Wallace but not by the letter I'd written him. I called him and told him he ought to get out. He was so nice about it I almost backed up. I just don't understand the man. . . . The reaction to firing Henry is terrific. The stock market went up twenty points. I've had an avalanche of telegrams from Maine to California agreeing with the action. . . . Anyway it's done.[22]

The result of Bess Truman's quiet advocacy to remove Henry Wallace had an impact after a full week of tough decision making on the president's part.

Another of Mrs. Truman's behind-the-scenes contributions was less political but much more important. When Harry became president, the budget for the National Institutes of Health was a meager $2 million—not surprising because the days of the war on cancer and other deadly diseases had not arrived, and most of America's money was going to fund World War II.[23]

During the 1948 campaign, Bess had met Florence Mahoney, an influential health advocate. Mahoney had become interested in the politics of America's health through her friendship with Mary Lasker, a philanthropist widow of an advertising executive who had contributed millions to medical research. Mahoney suggested to Mrs. Truman that the National Institutes of Health could become the headquarters for a massive effort to conquer diseases like cancer. Bess thought this was a fascinating idea, and she went to work on making it a reality. For the next four years, at budget time, the first lady urged the president to increase the NIH funding. Her advocacy paid off. By the time President Truman left office, the NIH had obtained $46 million from the federal government, a twentyfold increase.[24]

Bess Truman's interests and influence went beyond domestic politics to include foreign policy matters. For example, she supported her husband's formulation of the Truman Doctrine of 1947, championed Secretary of State George C. Marshall's proposal for the Marshall Plan, and paid careful attention to smaller foreign relations policies, such as the president's approval of a $10 million loan to Saudi Arabia for the construction of a railroad. In late summer 1946, Harry told Bess about his meeting with the finance minister of Saudi Arabia:

> I interviewed the finance minister of Saudi Arabia—a real old Biblical Arab with chin whiskers, a white gown, gold braid and everything. He is the most powerful man in the Arabian Gov't next to the old King. We had a most pleasant visit discussing his application for a ten million dollar loan from the Export-Import Bank, guaranteed by the Arabian-American Oil Company. He told me he wanted to build a railroad across the Arabia desert from the Red Sea to the Persian Gulf.[25]

The Arabian-American Oil Company had been organized in 1944. Known as Aramco, it was a highly production-oriented organization made up of geologists, petroleum engineers, and drilling crews that had a talent for operating in a radically different cultural environment like Saudi Arabia.[26]

King Abd al-Aziz of Saudi Arabia was interested in obtaining a large oil income as well as modernizing within the framework of an Islamic state. His interests ran parallel with the interests and proclivities of the Aramco team, and the king did all he could to ensure a political environment in which Aramco's production crews could grow.[27]

Aramco's personnel became the most effective advocates within the American government for increased production, cultural accommodation, and a fair share of the profits for Abd al-Aziz. Aramco also had constructed a pipeline from the Persian Gulf to the Mediterranean to send Saudi oil to Western refineries, and they had given Abd al-Aziz 50–50 profit sharing from all oil produced. By the time Harry S. Truman became president, a wide variety of technical, educational, and medical programs had been established in Saudi Arabia, and they greatly expanded in the postwar period. The proposed construction of a railroad across the Arabian desert from the Red Sea to the Persian Gulf was Abd al-Aziz's newest plan for modernization, and he had sent his finance minister to discuss the application for the loan with President Truman.[28]

Bess Truman had known about Aramco and its arrangement with Saudi Arabia since Harry's Senate years. When she returned to Washington, Harry discussed with her the Saudi application with the Export-Import Bank. She thought it was a good proposal and suggested that Harry write a letter to the bank's president in support of the loan. He eventually did so, and the railroad loan was approved in November 1946.[29]

It took a year and a half after the end of World War II before President Truman was willing to take a firm stand against the Soviet Union. He had discussed the matter with the first lady on several occasions, and she had suggested that he needed to make a major foreign policy speech. In February 1947, events unfolded that made the Truman Doctrine a reality, and Bess Truman's suggestion for a speech proved to be correct.

On 21 February 1947, a formal message from the British ambassador, Lord Inverchapel, was delivered to the State Department. Secretary of State George C. Marshall had been out of town. So it was

Undersecretary Dean Acheson who telephoned President Truman. Great Britain, under extreme financial hardship since World War II, could no longer provide economic and military support for Greece and Turkey. The British would withdraw 40,000 troops from Greece, and all economic assistance would end as of 31 March. It was hoped that the United States would assume the responsibility.[30]

Truman knew the British withdrawal from Greece would leave a void because their troops and money had helped maintain a royalist government in the middle of a civil war with Communist guerrillas. Simultaneously, the Soviets had refused to evacuate the northern provinces of Iran and neighboring Turkey, and they demanded a change in the Montreux convention governing the Turkish straits into a joint military occupation. Turkey had a long border with the USSR, and the Soviets were flexing their muscle.[31]

When Marshall returned to Washington on the following Monday, he and Acheson met with the president and urged "immediate action" to help Greece, and to a lesser degree Turkey. Marshall saw the situation as extremely serious. Truman agreed. Greece would have to be helped quickly, and with substantial sums.[32]

There followed a series of quick actions. First, the Cabinet gave immediate approval. Then the president called a meeting to inform congressional leaders of the need for a $400 million appropriation. Acheson told them that Greece was the rotten apple that would infect the whole barrel. "The Soviet Union was playing one of the greatest gambles in history at minimal cost," Acheson emphasized. When Acheson finished, Republican senator Arthur Vandenberg told the president that the best approach with Congress was to "scare the hell out of the country." His implication was that aid to Greece and Turkey could be had only if the president shocked Congress into action.[33]

That evening, Harry informed Bess about his meeting with congressional leaders. She agreed; a speech pointing out the Soviet threat would jolt Congress. "Who would write the speech?" she asked. Harry then handed her a seventy-nine-page report that had been written in 1946 by George Elsey of the White House staff and White House counsel Clark Clifford. It was titled "American Relations with the Soviet Union." Harry wanted Bess to read the report and give her opinion on whether it would serve as the origin for the speech.

The Clifford–Elsey report began by stating that the gravest problem facing the United States was that Soviet leaders appeared to be "on a course of aggrandizement designed to lead to eventual world domination by the USSR." In reviewing the situation in the Middle East, the report noted that the Soviets had hoped for the withdrawal of troops from Greece to establish another of their "friendly" governments there. The Soviet desire for Turkey was for it to be a puppet state to serve as a springboard for the domination of the eastern Mediterranean. Finally, the report concluded that besides maintaining its military strength, the United States "should support and assist all democratic countries which are in any way endangered by the USSR."[34]

Mrs. Truman read the Clifford–Elsey report the next day and told the president it was excellent. He was correct, she said; the report should provide the guiding principles for his speech to Congress. Bess Truman's input thus led to the development of the Truman Doctrine.

The first draft of the speech was prepared by the State Department, but President Truman thought it too wordy and technical. He also wanted the addition of a strong statement of American policy. Acheson made several cuts and revisions, and Mrs. Truman modified several passages. They both retained what had been in the Clifford–Elsey report about helping countries in jeopardy from the Soviet Union, except the Soviet Union was not mentioned by name.[35]

"It is the policy of the United States to support free peoples who are resisting attempted subjugation by armed minorities or by outside pressures," the line read originally. Bess changed it to: "I believe it must be the policy of the United States." She also added: "Should we fail to aid Greece and Turkey in this fateful hour, the effect will be far reaching to the West as well as to the East. We must take immediate and resolute action."

The speech setting forth the Truman Doctrine was delivered before a joint session of Congress on 12 March 1947. It was a simple declarative statement that lasted approximately eighteen minutes. Two days later, while resting in Key West, Harry wrote Bess:

> Hope the result of the message will be for world peace. It was a terrific step to take and one I've been worrying about ever since Marshall took over the State Dept. Our very first conversation

> was what to do about Russia in China, Korea and the Near East. . . . It was pleasing the way the Congress reacted—didn't you think it was nearly unanimous?[36]

On 22 April 1947, the Senate overwhelmingly approved aid to Greece and Turkey by a vote of 67 to 23. On 9 May, the House passed the bill by a margin of nearly three to one, 287 to 107. On 22 May, while visiting his mother in Grandview, President Truman signed the $400 million aid package. With it, the Truman Doctrine had been sanctioned.[37]

While President Truman was pushing the Greek–Turkish aid bill through Congress, he was receiving more dire reports about the condition of the other nations of Western Europe. The worst winter in Europe's history, with months of freezing temperatures and snow followed by spring floods, had all but wiped out the modest postwar recovery of England, France, Italy, and the other European nations. Of great concern was the British situation. On 1 August 1947, the president received a report from Secretary Marshall informing him that the British had drawn nearly $3 billion of the loan the United States had made them the previous summer, leaving less than $1 billion in their account. This meant that in another six months, the British would be bankrupt. Lewis Douglas, ambassador to Great Britain, wrote the president: "We run the serious risk of losing most of Western Europe if the crisis here develops as it now seems almost certain to develop."[38]

When Harry showed Marshall's report to Bess, she reacted with shock and sadness. It was time, she told him, for America to financially come to the rescue of Western Europe. He agreed, but the problem was convincing a Republican Congress to approve a massive aid bill. Bess suggested that Congress might be more willing to appropriate the billions needed if the program was associated with Secretary of State Marshall.

Two months later, speaking at Harvard's graduation ceremony, Secretary Marshall spelled out the details of the aid program that bore his name: the Marshall Plan. He emphasized that it was not a program of relief but of revival, not an offer of continuous support but of temporary cooperation. He also declared that the initiative and the responsibility for the plan had to be a joint effort. The

United States wanted Europe's best thinking on how the money should be spent. Marshall concluded by leaving the door open for the cooperation of the Soviet Union and its satellite states.[39]

During the summer of 1947, as sixteen European nations were meeting in Paris to draw up a comprehensive statement of their needs, President Truman and his aides were discussing in the White House what the program should be called. Clark Clifford suggested "the Truman Plan." Truman replied: "Are you crazy? If we send it up to that Republican Congress with my name on it, they'll tear it apart." He immediately thought of Bess's suggestion to name it after George C. Marshall. "We're going to call it the Marshall Plan," he declared.[40]

On 30 September, Harry wrote Bess several details about financing the Marshall Plan:

> Sent letters to Bridges, Vandenberg and Eaton requesting them to call their committees together as soon as possible. Had my food committee together and will make a radio speech Sunday. To feed France and Italy this winter will cost 580 million, the Marshall Plan 16 billion. . . . The 16 is for a four year period and is for peace. A Russian war would cost 400 billion and untold lives, mostly civilian. So I must do what I can.[41]

In early October, President Truman received the report from the Paris conference, and he summoned a special session of Congress to enact the Marshall Plan without delay. On 17 November, Congress met in response to the president's summons. Truman told them that the Marshall Plan called for a total outlay of $17 billion, with an appropriation of $6.8 billion needed by 1 April 1948 to enable Europe to survive the next fifteen months. By March 1948, large bipartisan majorities in both Houses appropriated the installment, and on 3 April, President Truman signed into law the European Recovery Act.[42]

The Soviet Union's reaction to the Marshall Plan was brutal. Throughout Europe, Stalin sent orders to his Communist leaders to redouble their efforts to seize power before the plan could begin to work. The possibility of civil war in Italy and France was discussed in the White House. The Italian government, suffering from a severe food shortage, appealed desperately for immediate shipment of all supplies. Then in February 1948, as Congress was still debating the Marshall Plan, the government of Czechoslovakia was toppled by a Communist coup.[43]

The Korean War, according to Harry S. Truman, was his "most important decision as President." And Mrs. Truman's advice at the onset of the war proved to be correct. The war began after Harry flew to Independence on 24 June 1950 to celebrate his thirty-first wedding anniversary. It was, in keeping with Bess's wishes, a quiet visit. The Wallaces and the Trumans gathered at 219 North Delaware for a family reunion. After dinner they sat out on the back porch, which Bess had widened and screened in earlier that year. At about 10:00 P.M., they decided to retire to the library. They were barely settled when Harry received a telephone call from Washington. He returned to the library with a grim look on his face. "That was Dean Acheson," he said. "The Communists have invaded South Korea." Bess sensed instantly that it meant war. "Oh, Harry," she said.[44]

President Truman told Acheson that he would return to Washington at once, but Acheson persuaded him to wait until the State Department could appraise the situation. Acheson recommended that the United States request an emergency meeting of the U.N. Security Council to declare that North Korea had committed an act of aggression and call for a cease-fire. Truman agreed. The next morning, Harry and Bess discussed the North Korean attack on South Korea. She was concerned that if the Communists were allowed to force their way into the Republic of Korea without opposition from the free world, it would mean a third world war. Harry hoped that the cease-fire resolution would stop hostilities, but Bess thought that the only recourse the United States had was to commit troops to Korea. That afternoon, Acheson called Truman a second time. He told the president that the U.N. Security Council would meet early that evening. He also informed Truman that the attack had been confirmed and that the South Korean front was disintegrating. Truman told Acheson that he would fly to Washington at once, and he asked him to provide a list of criteria for his review.[45]

Truman had a series of hectic conferences in the Blair House, but he still found time to write Bess on 26 June:

> We had a grand trip back after we were in the air. . . . The crowd at the Washington Airport was made up of the Secretaries of State and Defense and Army, Navy, and Air. . . . My conference was a most successful one, and there is a chance that things may work out without the necessity of mobilization. Haven't been so badly upset since Greece and Turkey fell into our lap. Let's hope for the best. . . . Lots and lots of love and many happy returns for the thirty-first year of your ordeal with me. It's been all pleasure for me.[46]

Two days after the North Korean invasion, Truman informed congressional leaders that the United States would take firm action in Korea. When he finally met with his National Security Council on 28 and 29 June, he requested that it recommend the deployment of American ground troops to South Korea, allowing General Douglas MacArthur to use American troops under his command in Japan for combat. In addition, Truman directed a naval blockade of North Korea. "Friday's decisions," according to Acheson's recollections, "were the culminating ones of a momentous week. We were then fully committed to Korea."[47] Harry S. Truman had not forgotten his wife's warning that if the free world did not stop the North Korean Communists, it could lead to World War III.

Mrs. Truman also played a critical role in the president's decision not to run for reelection. Shortly after Harry's victory in 1948, Bess asked him if he planned to run again in 1952. "I'm against another term," he told her. The third term, he thought, nearly killed Roosevelt, and the fourth was his demise.[48] Bess was greatly relieved; she did not want Harry to endure more than eight years in the White House. She wanted him to remain healthy and retire comfortably.

On 16 April 1950, President Truman wrote one of his most important memoranda: "I am not a candidate for nomination by the Democratic Convention. . . . In my opinion, eight years as President is enough and sometimes too much for any man to serve in that capacity."[49]

In November 1951, while Harry was vacationing in Key West, he took the memorandum out and read it to his staff. He wanted them to know his decision, he said, so they could plan their careers ahead of time. Nevertheless, he made it clear that he had no intention of making the announcement public for quite some time.[50]

The emergence of Dwight D. Eisenhower as the most likely Republican candidate made Truman feel urgent about finding a Democratic candidate, early in 1952. The more he thought about it, the more he became convinced that Governor Adlai Stevenson of Illinois was the man. At fifty-one, Stevenson was relatively young. He was progressive, the governor of an industrial state, a champion of honest government, a graduate of Princeton, and eloquent, witty, and urbane. Truman asked Stevenson to come and see him on 22 January 1952. He spoke to Stevenson about the office of the presidency, then asked him to run, saying that he need only agree and the nomination was his. But Stevenson voiced reluctance about running. Apparently, he did not want to be Harry S. Truman's handpicked candidate, and preferred being drafted by the Democratic convention.[51]

In the meantime, Truman was left without a candidate. For a few weeks, he reconsidered his decision not to run again. He convened a large meeting, which included the whole White House staff and several congressional leaders. At this meeting, Truman polled the entire room and asked each man what he thought. They gave varying reasons, but not one of them thought he should run again.[52]

Bess felt the same way. One evening, she sat down with Harry in his study and informed him that she could not survive another four years. She did not think he could either. She pointed out that if he ran and won, he would be seventy-three by the time he left office.[53]

A few days later, Matt Connelly, Truman's appointment secretary, arrived at the White House from a party given by Les Biffle, the secretary of the Senate. Biffle and everyone else at the party criticized Adlai Stevenson's reluctance to run and dismissed him as a candidate. They all said Harry Truman was the only man who could defeat General Eisenhower. Connelly found the president working late in his office and he told him what they were saying at the Biffle party. Truman quietly listened and said, "Do you think the old man will have to run again?" Connelly's face grew somber and he pointed to a portrait of Bess on the wall. "Would you do that to her?" he asked. Truman looked at the portrait. "All right," he said. "That settles it."[54]

By spring of 1952, Bess and Harry decided the time had come for Harry to inform the nation of his decision about running. He was the principal speaker at the Jefferson-Jackson Day dinner, a huge, annual $100-a-plate black-tie gathering of Democrats held the evening of 29 March at the National Armory. At the end of his address, he said: "I shall not be a candidate for reelection. I have served my country long and I think efficiently and honestly. I shall not accept a renomination. I do not feel that it is my duty to spend another four years in the White House."[55]

For a few seconds, the large audience sat silent in confusion. Then followed a mixture of applause and shouted cries of "No." "They were stunned," recalled Sam Rayburn. "Couldn't believe what they just heard. When Harry finished, he looked directly at Bess, who was sitting near the podium. He nodded at her as if to say, "Well, I did it!" She looked both happy and proud. There was the tiniest smile on her lips as if to say, "No, I did it!"[56]

Secretary of the Treasury John Snyder also saw Bess that evening. "I could tell that she was relieved that Harry had publicly released the news," he said. "Until that moment she thought he might try to convince her that he was the only possible candidate who could win. But he hadn't."[57]

Mrs. Truman's tenure as first lady was full of advice to her husband. Decisions like who should be chief justice of the United States to whether Harry should run for reelection were just a few important matters that her input influenced. There was a sign on President Truman's desk: "The Buck Stops Here." However, the buck did not stop there. He packed it in his briefcase every night, took it upstairs to his study, and discussed it with "the Boss." The Truman partnership was one of the closest in the history of the presidency, and Bess always played the role of partner and counselor in all decisions and all matters, great and small. She was without a doubt one of the most influential first ladies in American history.

CHAPTER 6

RETIREMENT

Late 1952 was a time of farewells. On 1 December, Bess Truman took Mamie Eisenhower on a tour of the White House. Compared to the bristling communications between the president and president elect, they had a pleasant visit. Mrs. Eisenhower wrote Mrs. Truman a note the day after she returned to New York, thanking her for her "graciousness." Days later, the women's press corps held a farewell luncheon for Bess, proving that they harbored no grudge for all the first lady's "no comments." One of the members read a lengthy poem, and the opening stanza noted that for them Mrs. Truman would always be "far more than a figure in history." The poem went on to praise her:

> We will think of you, rather, as a friend,
> Whose kindnesses never seemed to end. . . .
> And your wonderful way with a White House guest,
> Who might be nervous at such a test,
> And who probably never even knew
> That the feeling of ease was due to you—
> To your tact and kindness and savoir-faire
> Which made hard things easy when you were there.[1]

On 20 January 1953, Dwight D. Eisenhower took the oath of office. Bess Truman had been first lady for seven years and nine months, and at noon, it was over. She tried to pay attention to Eisenhower's inaugural address, but her mind was on a farewell luncheon at Secretary of State Dean Acheson's home, and later, catching their train for Independence.

As the Eisenhower inaugural parade made its way down Pennsylvania Avenue, the Trumans were being driven in a limousine back from the Capitol toward Georgetown. They arrived at the Achesons' home for lunch. It was a private affair for Cabinet members, White House aides, and a few close friends. As the car turned on P Street, a crowd of several hundred people cheered them. By the time the luncheon broke up, the P Street crowd had grown one block long, and traffic was backed up far beyond. Bess was astonished. When the Trumans went for their train at Union Station, thousands of Washingtonians were there to see them, wave, cheer, and call out "Good luck, Harry!" The *Ferdinand Magellan,* provided by the new president, had been attached to a B&O train bound for Missouri. The police had to form a flying wedge to get the Trumans through the crowd. "This is the greatest demonstration that any man could have, because I'm just Mr. Truman, private citizen now," Harry said from the rear platform. "I'll never forget it if I live to be a hundred." With the crowd singing "Auld Lang Syne," the train pulled slowly out of the station. Bess was beaming. It had been a long road to the White House, and now she was going home.[2]

In town after town, at every stop along the way through West Virginia, Ohio, Indiana, and Illinois, crowds swarmed the train to pay homage to the Trumans. As a result, the train was late when they pulled into the Missouri Pacific depot at Independence the night of 21 January. There they received a warm greeting. A crowd of 10,000, a fourth of Independence's population in 1953, greeted them, and the Kansas City American Legion Band struck up the "Missouri Waltz." Bess was so moved by the reception that she grasped a microphone that was handed to her and started to speak. But she was too choked up to say much. The crowd understood. Throughout the depot people were yelling, whistling, and crying at the same time.[3]

When the Trumans arrived at 219 North Delaware Street, there was another crowd of approximately 1,500 waiting. By this time Bess had regained her composure. As they entered the house, she said to

Harry: "If this is what you get for all those years of hard work, I suppose it was worth it."[4]

The reason the Trumans had come back to Independence and the old house was that financially, they had no other choice. To Harry's amazement, Bess had proposed that they rent an apartment in Washington and live there most of the time. She had become fond of life in the nation's capital, where she had made so many friends.[5] But Harry had left the presidency with no income and no support from the federal government, other than his army pension of $112 a month. He was provided with no expense money for secretarial help or office space, and although he and Bess had been able to save part of his $100,000-a-year salary as president during his second term, it was a modest amount. Bess was not wealthy either. The estate of Madge Wallace, not including the house, only totaled $33,000, which, after being divided four ways among Bess and her brothers, left Bess with a cash inheritance of $8,385. Congress finally passed a law in 1958 providing former presidents with a $25,000 annual pension, and money for staff and office space.[6]

Harry had received a number of offers from organizations for jobs paying over $100,000 a year, but he turned them down. John Snyder, former secretary of the treasury and a close friend of the Trumans, recalled:

> The phone began ringing at once. Lots of calls were job offers: the chairmanship of several big companies—a sewing machine company, a railroad, a clothing store chain, a movie company. All had six-figure salaries and a few hours of work. He and Bess saw through them right away; it wasn't Harry Truman they were interested in, but the prestige of the ex-President.[7]

Harry and Bess also quickly discovered that they missed the White House. "You can't always be as you want to be after you've been under those bright lights," Harry told a reporter. He missed the bright lights and the pace of the presidency. He felt strange without the daily constant pressures.[8] When Bess was interviewed by Washington's *This Week* magazine and asked whether she missed the White House, she replied,

> I miss certain aspects of my job as First Lady. It was a challenging, intensely interesting position, and I rather enjoyed tackling its many problems. . . . Here in Independence we have a 12-room, three-story house and it would be extremely pleasant to have some of the wonderful staff we had in the White House to help run it. I certainly miss them. We only have our maid, who has been with us for 28 years, and occasional cleaning help.[9]

Vietta Garr made a daily trip to 219 North Delaware to do the cooking, which helped Bess manage the household. Arthritis in Bess's hands suddenly worsened, handicapping her efforts to cook and clean. There was another notable change: for the first time in the fifty years Bess had spent in that house, her mother was no longer there. The mixture of loneliness and boredom ended up turning her into a world-class traveler.[10]

Soon after the Trumans had returned to Independence, oilman Ed Pauley invited them to vacation on his estate on little Coconut Island in Hawaii. Bess took Harry by surprise with an announcement that she thought it would be a good idea to accept the invitation. She also asked Margaret to join them for what turned out to be a month-long trip.[11] On 18 March 1953, Bess wrote Mary Paxton Keeley about their plans and her problems with arthritis:

> We are about to take off for the Pacific and I hate to leave the house looking as it does. We have never finished unpacking and getting things settled. Maybe never will. I have acquired an old age ailment—arthritis—and am somewhat handicapped on doing things with my hands. Hope to see you when we get back.[12]

The trip to Hawaii turned out to be one of the best vacations Bess had ever had. They traveled by train to San Francisco aboard Averell Harriman's private railroad and sailed on the *President Cleveland,* of the American Presidents Line, to Hawaii. Most of their time was spent lounging on the beach at Pauley's estate in Kaneohe Bay. They also drove to Honolulu through the Pali Pass on Oahu and flew to the big island of Hawaii in a navy C-47 to see the great volcanoes Mauna Loa and Mauna Kea. Bess had the chance to enjoy some deep-sea fishing excursions.[13]

The Hawaiian vacation marked only the beginning of the Trumans' trips during the 1950s. Harry had bought Bess a new car, a four-door black Chrysler, but she dared him to drive it for much of any distance. Upon their return from Hawaii, he bought a car for himself, a two-tone green Dodge coupe. Harry wanted to give the car "a real tryout," so he proposed that he and Bess drive to Washington. Bess liked the idea, thinking that it would be fun to be on their own again. The Trumans had not traveled on their own by automobile in nine years, the last time being a return trip from the Chicago convention in 1944.[14]

Off they went in early June 1953. They had discussed who would do the driving and worked out a compromise: Harry would be behind the wheel, but he would drive much slower than normal. They had only gone a short distance when Bess chastised him for speeding. Harry insisted he was only going fifty-five. "Do you think I'm losing my eyesight?" Bess said. "Slow down!" Truman wrote in his book, *Mr. Citizen,* that at fifty-five miles an hour, other cars soon started passing them. "They had a chance to look us over," he wrote. "Pretty soon the shouted greetings started."[15]

The Trumans got as far as Hannibal, Missouri, before they found out how difficult being on their own was going to be. While having lunch in Hannibal, two former county judges recognized them, and suddenly all the customers in the restaurant had to shake hands and get autographs. In Decatur, Illinois, 150 miles later, they asked a gas station attendant for directions to a motel. He recognized them and notified the chief of police, who sent two plainclothes men and four uniformed police to guard them. They took Harry and Bess to dinner and to breakfast the next morning, and escorted them out of town. While driving the Pennsylvania Turnpike, a state trooper pulled them over because he wanted to shake hands. The incident prompted the newspapers to report that Harry Truman had gotten a ticket. At the hotel where they stopped in Wheeling, West Virginia, the lobby was packed with reporters. The Trumans had a wonderful time in Washington that summer, and the good time continued when they drove to New York to visit Margaret. But it was their last venture by automobile.[16]

It was anything but serene when the Trumans returned to Independence. As they pulled into their driveway, they saw a woman kneeling in the backyard picking Bess's beautiful white tulips.[17] One of the first things Bess had planned to do when she returned home was take down an iron fence that the Secret Service had put up around 219 North Delaware. The Trumans had only been at home a few days before she decided it was not a good idea. Approximately 5,000 people a week walked or drove past the house, and the fence was their primary protection from souvenir hunters.[18]

Harry and Bess also left Washington without a Secret Service detail. At that time, the United States was not concerned with the welfare of its ex-presidents. The city of Independence provided them the protection of one policeman, but he was not on duty all day and all night.[19]

People peered at Harry and Bess every time they left their house, and sightseeing buses cruised along North Delaware Street almost all day. In 1955, Margaret Truman interviewed her parents for the CBS *Person to Person* television show, and Bess confirmed that crowd control had become a problem:

> MARGARET: Are we still getting a lot of sightseers and visitors?
> BESS: Oh, loads of them, yes.
> MARGARET: All the time?
> BESS: All the time. Every day. We had a funny experience the other night. Dad and I went over to see your cousins across the street and there were so many out here in front of the house we couldn't come home. We had to spend most of the evening on the front porch all by ourselves because our cousins weren't at home.[20]

The throngs of sightseers did not deter Harry S. Truman from taking his regular morning walk. He would leave at 6:45 A.M. for a stroll around town and return at 7:30 for breakfast. One winter morning, Harry left the house without noticing that the streets were covered with ice. He slipped and cracked four ribs. One thing changed in his routine as a result of the misadventure. Bess issued an order forbidding him to go out for a morning walk when there was snow or ice on the ground.[21]

Every workday morning at 8:15, Harry would emerge from the back porch carrying a briefcase. He would get in his Dodge and drive to Kansas City, where he had established an office in the Federal Reserve Bank Building. There he set about writing his memoirs, which took up much of his time. The due date for the manuscript was 30 June 1955. Doubleday was the publisher. Harry eventually went through four assistants who helped him write the two-volume work.[22]

By early 1955, the manuscript totaled two million words, but Doubleday's editor in chief, Ken McCormick, asked that it be cut to 580,000 words. The revisions became a tiresome task for Harry, and he called on Dean Acheson to go over the whole accumulation. McCormick, however, thought that Bess had played a significant role because Harry seemed to make better decisions about the manuscript after having talked with her at home in the evenings. "She was his true North, I think," McCormick later recalled.[23] Harry paid tribute to Bess's preparation of the book in the preface: "I owe a great deal of gratitude to Mrs. Truman, on whose counsel and judgment I frequently called."[24] For all the work, Harry made very little money from the book. He received no royalties, only a lump sum of $600,000, of which he had to pay 67 percent in taxes. He calculated that he earned $37,000 after he had provided for his assistants.[25]

What finally freed Harry and Bess from financial worries was the 600-acre Truman farm in Grandview. Early in Truman's presidency, a group of Jackson County friends had bought the farm from Truman's mother, planning to preserve it as a historic site. In 1946, Harry decided to purchase it from them. Ten years later, he sold most of the acreage to a real estate developer for a shopping center called Truman Corners. The deal ended all financial worries for Harry's brother, Vivian, and sister Mary as well.[26]

In 1954, the city of Independence offered a large tract of Slover Park as a site for the Harry S. Truman Library. The location was only about one mile from 219 North Delaware Street. Harry accepted his first check for the library from the Independence Chamber of Commerce on 22 July 1954 while Bess stood in the background and smiled proudly. Although offers had come from the University of Missouri and others, Bess had pushed for an Independence site.[27]

The library became the focus of the Trumans' interest for several years. The United States government contributed nothing for the library. Harry raised all the money himself. With Bess by his side, he made speeches and attended fund-raising dinners around the country. In a year and a half he raised more than $1 million of the $1.75 million needed for the building.[28]

On 8 May 1955, Truman's seventy-first birthday, over 2,000 people gathered at Slover Park to watch Harry turn the first spade of earth at a groundbreaking ceremony for the library. After the ceremony, Bess hosted a buffet dinner at home for nearly 150 people. It was a sight Margaret Truman never thought she would see. There Bess "stood at the door of her sanctuary, greeting each guest as he or she entered the vestibule." Guests ate at tables in the yard, and the dessert was a birthday cake shaped like the yet-to-be-built library.[29]

In mid-March 1956, Margaret announced that she was engaged to be married to Elbert Clifton Daniel Jr., who was an assistant foreign news editor of the *New York Times*. Margaret and Clifton, as he was called, had known each other since November 1955. Bess first learned about Clifton when he sent Margaret flowers and telegrams during the 1955 Christmas season. Margaret called her mother in January to tell her about the engagement. Soon after, Harry and Bess made a trip to New York to meet their future son-in-law.[30]

The wedding took place on 21 April in the little Trinity Episcopal Church in Independence, where Bess Wallace and Captain Harry Truman had been married in 1919. Margaret wore a pale beige wedding gown with a butterfly-pleated tulle skirt fashioned of two-hundred-year-old Venetian lace. Harry and Bess arrived by limousine with Margaret. Only immediate family members and a few close friends attended. It was followed by a small reception at 219 North Delaware, where Margaret and Clifton cut a four-tiered white cake decorated with sugar carnations. Harry and Bess greeted their guests in the comfortable front hall, and Vietta Garr served them champagne. Guests were also treated to a big roast turkey, sliced Missouri ham, beaten biscuits, small sandwiches in rainbow colors, and an assortment of olives, nuts, candies, and mints. The reception was held indoors, but outside, hundreds of reporters and photographers gathered at the iron gate.[31]

Less than a month after, Harry and Bess departed on a seven-week tour of Europe. The primary reason for the trip was an invitation to Harry to accept an honorary degree at Oxford. Bess had long wanted to travel abroad. For her it was the trip of a lifetime, and her first venture overseas.[32]

On 11 May 1956, the Trumans sailed from New York on the SS *United States,* accompanied by Stanley Woodward, who had been Harry's chief of protocol, and his wife, Sara. They landed at Le Havre and went directly by train to Paris. By 17 May, their first full day in Paris, reporters dogged them wherever they went. They arrived in Rome on 21 May, the beginning of three weeks of travel through Italy. They visited all of Rome's ancient monuments, had an audience with Pope Pius XII, saw Mount Vesuvius and the ruins of Pompeii, and visited Naples, Florence, and Venice.[33]

The Trumans traveled from Italy to Salzburg, Austria, and Bonn, West Germany, then swung back through France again, stopping at Versailles. They arrived in Brussels on 13 June and The Hague the following day. On 17 June, they were on their way to England, crossing the English Channel on the night boat. The highlight of the trip occurred when Harry received an honorary degree of doctor of civil law from Oxford on 20 June. Four days later, Harry and Bess had lunch with Sir Winston Churchill and Lady Churchill at Chartwell, the Churchill family estate forty miles south of London. On 26 June, they joined Queen Elizabeth II and the Duke of Edinburgh at Buckingham Palace for lunch. On 28 June, from Southampton, the Trumans sailed for home, their European tour over.[34]

Back in Independence by 5 July, and scarcely unpacked, Harry plunged into election-year politics. He was determined to see Averell Harriman, rather than Adlai Stevenson, secure the Democratic nomination. Harriman had been elected governor of New York two years earlier. He also had strong foreign policy credentials, having been an envoy for FDR and Truman in dealing with the Soviet Union. At the Chicago convention in August, it soon became apparent that Stevenson's delegates had control and Harriman did not have a chance. Despite this reality, Harry called a press conference and announced that he was backing Harriman anyway. Stevenson "lacks the kind of fighting spirit we need to win," Truman charged. Bess was not pleased. She immediately sought out Tom Evans, the Kansas City businessman who had been on the inside of the nomination for vice president in 1944. "Mrs. Truman, for the only time in my life, in Chicago, was quite upset about the attitude that Mr. Truman was taking regarding Stevenson," Evans recalled. "For the only time in my life I saw her upset, even in tears, pleading with me." Bess asked Evans, "Tom, can't you do something to stop Harry? He's making a fool of himself." Eventually, with the help of Evans, she persuaded Harry to withdraw his support of Harriman and endorse Stevenson. Despite his endorsement, President Eisenhower easily defeated Stevenson, leaving Truman frustrated.[35]

The year 1957 was an important one for the Trumans. On 5 June, in New York, Margaret had a baby boy. He was named Clifton Truman Daniel. Harry and Bess were on the train for New York the next morning. Bess had always wanted a son. Now she had a grandson. Her delight was completely private, of course. She had nothing to say to reporters. However, on 7 June, the *New York Times* carried a photograph of the proud grandparents at the hospital, looking through the nursery window at their grandson. Bess also wasted no time filling the mail with descriptions of the baby for the benefit of Mary Paxton Keeley and other friends. When little Clifton was eight months old, Bess proudly told Mary: "He weighs a little over 19 lbs now and is 28 in. long—one tooth! And seems to be a healthy youngster. Marg says he eats everything in sight. She doesn't half know what that means!"[36]

One month later, formal dedication of the Truman Library took place on 6 July. Harry was able to move out of the Federal Reserve Bank Building into an all-new office suite at the library. Harry used the same mahogany desk he had used in the Oval Study upstairs at the White House, and Rose Conway, his White House secretary, assisted him with letters and phone calls. He loved his office and was at the library almost every day, including Sundays, unless he was traveling.[37] Bess often showed up at the library by midmorning, in a house dress and flat shoes, to open and answer the mail for a few hours. By late 1959, she had become the official mail sorter after one of Harry's secretaries died. Bess explained her new routine to Mary Paxton Keeley in early 1960:

> The holidays nearly finished me and I gave up going to Phoenix and Wash. with Harry. I have been going to the office and sorting the horrible mail whenever I can and those days I don't get another thing done. One of his secretaries died last fall and Rose hasn't found anyone she wants to take his place.[38]

Before Bess became a part-time volunteer secretary at the library, she lived a leisurely life. She played bridge regularly with the Tuesday Bridge Club, made a weekly visit to see her hairdresser, Doris Miller, read four newspapers a day, and listened to baseball games on the radio. She also continued to travel. In 1958, the Trumans made a second trip to Europe—this time a much more private, second honeymoon to Italy and southern France. Bess wrote Katie Louchheim, vice chair of the Democratic National Committee, that she was "having one of those vacations of a lifetime." She emphasized that she especially enjoyed the French Riviera and the food: "This is my first time on the Riviera so you may know how much I am enjoying everything. However, I find this French food a bit hard on the waistline. Even so with all of our good time the old Goddess of Liberty will look mighty handsome to us."[39]

In late 1958, Bess found a lump in her left breast. She chose to ignore it and made the decision that she would live long enough to participate in two major events of 1959, the Democratic Party's salute to Harry's seventy-fifth birthday on 8 May in New York and the birth of her second grandchild. Despondent about her health, she quit traveling with Harry for a while. When he went to Washington for a weeklong birthday celebration, she went to New York to visit Margaret. Upon returning home, Bess wrote Katie Louchheim: "Harry had such a wonderful time with all of you that whole week. It made me very envious, but I must confess I had a happy time with my one grandson (so far!)."[40] By mid-May she had checked into the Research Hospital in Kansas City for surgery. The tumor had grown to the size of a grapefruit but was not cancerous. However, it had invaded the lymph nodes in her left arm, and Dr. Wallace Graham, who had left the White House to practice medicine in Kansas City, ordered a mastectomy. It took Bess a long time to recover from the operation and from the psychological pain a woman feels after losing a breast.[41]

On 19 May 1959, Margaret gave birth to William Wallace Daniel, lifting Bess's spirits. Within the next few years, she had two more grandsons: Harrison Gates Daniel and Thomas Washington Daniel. Bess doted on all four boys when they traveled to Independence to visit her. She let them call her "Gammy," and she could be counted on for several of Vietta Garr's brownies at any hour of the day. The

Trumans also provided a sandbox, swing, and jungle gym in their backyard so the boys could play outdoors.[42] Margaret remembered that some of the happiest times her sons had was when they visited Gammy and Grandpa at Christmastime:

> The boys love to visit their grandfather and grandmother in Independence. They especially like to go there for Christmas, when they are allowed to decorate the tree with all the ornaments I remember from my own childhood and hear stories of Christmases past. In Independence they have a lot of freedom.[43]

Democratic politics remained very much a part of the Trumans' lives, along with grandparenting. By 1960, a new generation of politicians was on the rise. With Eisenhower retiring and Richard Nixon the likely choice for a Republican nominee, the chance of a Democratic victory seemed promising. Of those Democrats in the running, Harry S. Truman's favorites were Senator Stuart Symington of Missouri and Senate Majority Leader Lyndon B. Johnson. Truman was not enthusiastic about John F. Kennedy because he considered Kennedy too young and inexperienced. Bess Truman thought her husband should remain neutral. "She refused to get excited about the Democratic Party and told Dad he was crazy if he went to another convention at the age of seventy-six," Margaret remembered. "Let the next generation fight it out among themselves—that was her attitude." Harry took her advice about not going to the convention, but later he joined the Kennedy campaign. The 1960 election was his last hurrah, and he covered nine states giving speeches, holding press conferences, and riding in parades. Bess remained behind in Independence during the summer and fall of 1960, but she silently hoped for a Democratic victory.[44]

Seven months after Kennedy's inauguration in 1961, the new president wrote Harry a letter inviting the Trumans back to the White House. Harry was scheduled to speak in Washington at the National Press Club on the thirteenth anniversary of his victory over Tom Dewey, and President Kennedy thought it would be a good time to honor him. "Mrs. Kennedy and I would be delighted to have you and Mrs. Truman spend the night with us at the White House prior to your speech," wrote Kennedy. Harry and Bess accepted.[45]

On 1 November 1961, Harry and Bess and Margaret and Clifton were guests at the White House for a dinner in the Trumans' honor and for an overnight visit. Many of Harry's former Cabinet members assembled for the occasion. They dined at the great horseshoe table, decorated with bronze and yellow chrysanthemums, and were served a dinner prepared by Mrs. Kennedy's French chef that included Mimosa salad, crab mousse, American grouse, braised celery, and petits fours. Eugene List, who had played for Truman at the 1945 Potsdam conference, provided after-dinner entertainment in the East Room. List performed a piano concert of Truman's favorite Mozart and Chopin compositions and then invited the former president to take a turn on the big Steinway. Mrs. Truman thought that Mrs. Kennedy made a charming hostess, and she was quite enthusiastic about Jackie's redecoration of the White House. The Trumans were deeply grieved by President Kennedy's assassination in 1963 because they had grown fond of the young president and his wife. When Harry heard the news, he became physically ill and took to his bed, leaving Bess to deal with reporters.[46]

After the assassination, a bill was passed by Congress authorizing Secret Service protection for former presidents. Shortly thereafter, a Secret Service detail arrived in Independence. Neither Harry nor Bess had any desire for the Secret Service to return to their lives. "Mother reacted as if they had just told her she was going to have to spend four more years in the White House," Margaret remembered. Bess simply refused to allow the agents on the property. Then Harry found the bill and discovered a clause in it allowing ex-presidents the right to refuse protection. The impasse was broken when President Lyndon Johnson called and had a talk with Bess. She finally agreed that the agents could guard Harry during the day, but she still would not allow them into the house.[47]

In October 1964, Harry fell in the upstairs bathroom, hitting his head on the edge of the tub and fracturing three ribs. The impact also shattered his eyeglasses, cutting him badly over the right eye. Bess called the police and an ambulance. Two days later, Dr. Wallace Graham announced that the former president's condition was satisfactory. Harry was home in a few days, but he never fully recovered from the fall. He became frail, he lost a lot of weight, and his face was drawn. Yet he continued taking his morning walks, and his routine at the library remained the same.[48]

Harry's slow recuperation was a difficult time for Bess. In 1965, when Mary Paxton Keeley had a show of photographs and paintings in Columbia, Missouri, Bess wrote to say they could not come. "We can't drive that far anymore," she explained to Mary. In March 1967, the Trumans flew to Key West for a two-week vacation with Margaret, Clifton, and the four boys. Bess loved being back in Key West, and she was excited about being able to travel again. She told Margaret that it was the first time they had left Independence in over two years. "It's the longest I have stayed home since 1934," she exclaimed. They made a return visit to Key West in 1968, but it would be their final trip.[49]

By 1969, old age began to take its toll on the Trumans. Bess was eighty-four and Harry was eighty-five. On 28 June 1969, they celebrated their fiftieth wedding anniversary quietly at home. A few close friends dropped by, but there was no party. Bess explained to reporters that President Truman was physically not up to standing for a long time shaking hands.[50]

Harry's health began to fail in 1972. On 5 December, he was hospitalized for lung congestion. Dr. Graham told reporters at Research Hospital that President Truman's condition was "very serious." Bess spent almost all her time at his bedside. On 14 December, he was no longer able to talk. By Christmas, he slipped into a coma and was near death. Bess had reached a point of total exhaustion, and Margaret persuaded her mother to go home with her to Independence. Margaret remembered: "Dad was in a coma and there was nothing we could do to help him. . . . She wanted to be with him even though he was no longer conscious. But it seemed, like many decisions made under stress, the right one at the time." At 7:52 the next morning, Dr. Graham called Bess to tell her that Harry had died.[51]

The army had planned a five-day state funeral for President Truman that entailed taking his body to Washington to lie in state in the Capitol rotunda and returning him to Missouri for burial. The plan conflicted with Bess's wishes. "Keep it simple, simple," Bess told Margaret and Clifton. They thus worked out a two-day ceremony, which would take place in Independence.[52]

Bess helped Margaret prepare a guest list for the funeral service held 28 December. Only 250 people were invited because space for the service in the Truman Library auditorium was limited. The body lay in state in the lobby of the Truman Library on 27 December, and approximately 75,000 people passed by the closed casket, including President and Mrs. Nixon and Lyndon and Lady Bird Johnson. After the funeral, Harry S. Truman was buried in the courtyard of the library. Six howitzers fired a twenty-one-gun salute, and taps was sounded. Afterward, the commanding general removed the flag that draped Truman's casket. He carefully folded it and presented it to Bess. She handed it to Margaret. Bess Truman then gave her last gift to Harry S. Truman. A soldier laid a blanket of red carnations, his favorite flower, on the casket.[53]

Margaret wanted her mother to come to New York to live with her, but Bess preferred to stay in Independence. The old house held many memories of Harry, Margaret, her mother, and her three younger brothers, and she was happy there. She also remained in close touch with friends, sharing problems and old memories. Within a year, the arthritis in her hands grew steadily worse, which made her writing "practically illegible," she told Mary Paxton Keeley. Therefore, the telephone became a more important form of communication, and she and Margaret would talk long distance three or four times a week. Bess also spent a lot of time reading books—large numbers of them. Her favorites included mysteries, biographies, and novels.[54]

Mrs. Truman remained interested in Democratic politics after President Truman's death. In 1972, she had written a sympathetic letter to vice presidential nominee Senator Tom Eagleton of Missouri after he was forced to withdraw from the race because he had undergone psychiatric treatment for depression. When Eagleton came up for reelection in 1974, he asked Bess to become honorary cochairman of his campaign. After discussing it with Margaret, Bess agreed. She was especially delighted that her cochair was Stan "The Man" Musial, one of the greatest baseball players of all time, who had played for the St. Louis Cardinals. Eagleton did not realize that the former first lady was an ex-third baseman until he visited her on the eve of the campaign. When the topic of baseball came up, Bess revealed to Eagleton her knowledge of the sport. Eagleton remembered: "She knew every player in the Kansas City Royals starting lineup and had very strong opinions of the plusses and minuses of each one." The Eagleton–Truman–Musial team easily won the election.[55]

Two years later, in 1976, Bess got another win with an endorsement. She issued a statement through her lawyer, Rufus Burrus, backing state senator Ike Skelton in his bid for the Fourth Congressional District seat. Her statement came from her hospital room at Research Medical Center, where she was receiving treatment for arthritis. Bess declared that she had known Skelton and his family for many years and was planning to get an absentee ballot so she could vote for him. Skelton had not run well in Jackson County during the primary, but with Mrs. Truman's support, he won the general election.[56]

Bess was the last living Wallace family member. Her brother, Fred, died in 1957 from a heart attack. Frank Wallace died in 1960 and George Wallace in 1963. Her sister-in-law, May Wallace, who lived only a few feet away on Van Horne Street, visited Bess often and was a cheerful connection to the past. On Mrs. Truman's ninety-sixth birthday, in 1981, May organized a large party that was attended by Bess's friends and associates from Independence.[57]

With Bess's advancing age came deteriorating health. After spending twenty-two days in the hospital with a bleeding ulcer in 1982, she returned home and experienced a stroke that left her unable to communicate. On 18 October 1982, at the age of ninety-seven, Mrs. Truman died of congestive heart failure at her home.[58]

Funeral services were held on 21 October at Trinity Episcopal Church, to which she had belonged for many years. Only 150 people were invited to attend. Mourners included her close friends and the maids and nurses who had cared for her. First Lady Nancy Reagan also attended Bess Truman's funeral, as well as former first ladies Betty Ford and Rosalynn Carter. Mrs. Truman, who lived longer than any other first lady, was buried beside her husband in the courtyard of the Truman Library, with the final line on her tombstone inscribed according to Harry S. Truman's will: "First Lady, the United States of America, April 12, 1945–January 20, 1953."[59]

Bess Truman's passing garnered headlines and condolences from around the world. President Ronald Reagan said: "She was a devoted wife, a loving mother, and a gracious, unassuming first lady. Bess Truman embodied the basic decency of America." The *Washington Post* published a full-page article simply entitled "Remembering Bess." Former president Jimmy Carter paid tribute by saying: "The loss is a great one to this nation, and we will miss the quiet dignity with which she devoted herself to her country, to her husband, and to her family."[60] Born in the Gilded Age, the age of the opening of the American West and Victorian ideals, Bess Wallace Truman had lived through two world wars, the beginning of the cold war, the Korean and Vietnam wars, and rocket trips to the moon. A woman of Midwestern nineteenth-century upbringing, she emerged in the twentieth century as a housewife who loved her family and protected her own privacy. As first lady in the uncertain post–World War II years, she was genuine, gracious, loyal, hardworking, thoughtful, Christian, dutiful, and dignified. These were the principal characteristics of the so-called Republican mother of the Revolutionary War, who practiced domestic virtue and shared a valued political sentiment: patriotism. The American public found her idea of womanhood a welcome relief from the unorthodox activism of Eleanor Roosevelt.

Thrust into the world of Washington politics and power before the days of professional image making, Bess Wallace Truman steadfastly remained what she wanted to be: a woman of middle-American values. Her public persona epitomized the post–World War II ideal of first ladies—that they should be seen and not heard. She had been reared to be a lady by a well-to-do Independence family, and she personified traditional ideas regarding 1940s and 1950s domesticity. But she also embraced the prevailing feminist ideas regarding women's organizations and volunteerism.

The full impact of Bess Wallace Truman's contribution to the history of America has been measured only in recent years. Her keen intelligence, calm reasoning, and unswerving devotion to her husband were rarely revealed to the American public because of her vision of her role as first lady: to stay in the background, showing herself only as a support for Harry S. Truman. Few people knew that she was his full partner, in every sense of the word.

NOTES

ABBREVIATION

HSTL Harry S. Truman Library

INTRODUCTION

1. For further analysis of the female dominion and its influence, see Robyn Muncy, *Creating a Female Dominion in American Reform, 1890–1935* (New York: Oxford University Press, 1991). For postwar feminism, see Nancy F. Cott, *The Grounding of Modern Feminism* (New Haven, Conn.: Yale University Press, 1987).

2. E. Clifton Daniel Oral History Interview, Oral History Collection, HSTL.

3. Katie Louchheim Oral History Interview, Oral History Collection, HSTL.

4. Dr. Wallace H. Graham Oral History Interview, Oral History Collection, HSTL.

5. Mary Paxton Keeley Oral History Interview, Oral History Collection, HSTL.

6. Frances Perkins Oral History Interview, Columbia University Oral History Project, Columbia University.

7. "'No Secret,' Truman Says of Wife's Job in the Senate," *New York Times,* 27 July 1944, 11.

8. Charles S. Murphy quotation in Gedrry Van der Heuvel, "Remembering Bess," *Washington Post,* 19 October 1982, D1.

CHAPTER 1: LADY FROM INDEPENDENCE

1. Margaret Truman, *Bess W. Truman* (New York: Macmillan, 1986), 228–229.

2. Ibid., 2–3.

3. Ibid.

4. Ibid.

5. Nancy Woloch, *Women and the American Experience* (Boston: McGraw Hill, 2006), 116–121.

6. Truman, *Bess W. Truman,* 3–4.

7. Ibid., 6, 14–16.

8. Mary Paxton Keeley, *Back in Independence* (Chillicothe, Mo.: Community Press, 1992), 97–99, 106–107.

9. Mary Paxton Keeley Oral History Interview, Oral History Collection, HSTL.

10. Truman, *Bess W. Truman,* 7–8; Jhan Robbins, *Bess and Harry: An American Love Story* (New York: G. P. Putnam, 1980), 19–20.

11. Mary Paxton Keeley Oral History Interview, Oral History Collection, HSTL.

12. Truman, *Bess W. Truman,* 11; David McCullough, *Truman* (New York: Simon & Schuster, 1992), 45–46.

13. McCullough, *Truman,* 37–46.

14. Harry S. Truman, *Memoirs:* Volume 1, *Year of Decisions* (New York: Doubleday, 1955), 116.

15. Truman, *Bess W. Truman,* 10.

16. Mary Paxton Keeley Oral History Interview, Oral History Collection, HSTL.

17. Truman, *Bess W. Truman,* 15.

18. Ibid., 17; Mary Paxton Keeley Oral History Interview, Oral History Collection, HSTL.

19. Truman, *Bess W. Truman,* 19. There were a number of first ladies with alcoholic fathers—Edith Roosevelt, Eleanor Roosevelt, and Jacqueline Kennedy. Edith Roosevelt's father also committed suicide.

20. Ibid., 19–20.

21. Ibid., 21–22.

22. Ibid.

23. Ibid., 30–31. There are numerous accounts of how their courtship began. For example, see McCullough, *Truman,* 80–81; and Robert H. Ferrell, *Harry S. Truman: A Life* (Columbia: University of Missouri Press, 1994), 50.

24. Quoted in Robbins, *Bess and Harry,* 24.

25. Ferrell, *Harry S. Truman,* 26–30.

26. Quoted in Robbins, *Bess and Harry,* 25.

27. Harry Truman to Bess Wallace, 22 June and 12 July 1911, in Robert H. Ferrell, *Dear Bess: The Letters from Harry to Bess Truman, 1910–1959* (New York: W. W. Norton, 1983), 39–41.

28. Truman, *Bess W. Truman,* 48–51.

29. Ibid., 55–56.

30. Ibid., 56–59; Ferrell, *Harry S. Truman,* 52–53.

31. Harry Truman to Bess Wallace, 8 July 1917, Papers of Harry S. Truman, Family Correspondence File, Box 15, HSTL.

32. Truman, *Bess W. Truman,* 70–74.

33. Harry Truman to Bess Wallace, 26 January 1919, in Ferrell, *Dear Bess,* 294.

34. Truman, *Bess W. Truman,* 79–81; McCullough, *Truman,* 143–145.

35. Quoted in Robbins, *Bess and Harry,* 33. For Madge Wallace's relationship with Harry Truman, see Ferrell, *Harry S. Truman,* 76–77.

36. Robbins, *Bess and Harry,* 34–36; McCullough, *Truman,* 145–148.

37. Only a few scholars have argued that Bess Truman was anti-Semitic. For example, see Michael Beschloss, *Presidential Courage: Brave Leaders and How They Changed America, 1789–1989* (New York: Simon & Schuster, 2007), 209–210.

38. Quoted in Robbins, *Bess and Harry,* 38.

39. McCullough, *Truman,* 158–159.

40. Robbins, *Bess and Harry,* 40–41.

41. Truman, *Bess W. Truman,* 92; McCullough, *Truman,* 168–169.

42. Truman, *Bess W. Truman,* 100–101.

43. Ibid., 113; McCullough, *Truman,* 188.

44. "Vietta Garr," National Park Service pamphlet, Washington, D.C., 2007.

45. Robbins, *Bess and Harry,* 44.

46. Truman, *Bess W. Truman,* 125–127.

47. Quote in ibid., 132.

48. Ibid., 133. See also *Kansas City Star,* 9 November 1934, 13.

49. "Meet Harry's Boss, Bess," *Collier's,* 12 February 1949, 14.

50. Bess Furman, "Bess Truman, Silent Partner," Bess Furman Papers, Library of Congress.

51. Truman, *Bess W. Truman,* 134–135.

52. Ibid., 139.

53. Ibid., 159–160.

54. Ibid., 178–179.

55. Quoted in Robbins, *Bess and Harry,* 58; Ferrell, *Harry S. Truman,* 150.

56. Quoted in Robbins, *Bess and Harry,* 58–59.

57. Ibid., 59; Truman, *Bess W. Truman,* 193.

58. Truman, *Bess W. Truman,* 198–199; McCullough, *Truman,* 256–259.

59. Truman, *Bess W. Truman,* 207–208.

60. Robbins, *Bess and Harry,* 64.

61. Quoted in Truman, *Bess W. Truman,* 215.

62. "Truman's Wife on U.S. Payroll, Got Raise, Too," "The Senator's Wife," Mary Paxton Keeley Papers, Clipping File, Box 1, HSTL.

63. Harry Truman to Bess Truman, 27 June 1942, in Ferrell, *Dear Bess,* 479–480.

64. Marianne Means, "What Three Presidents Say About Their Wives," *Good Housekeeping,* August 1962, 59.

65. McCullough, *Truman,* 306–307.

66. Tom Evans Oral History Interview, Oral History Collection, HSTL.

67. Truman, *Bess W. Truman,* 234–235.

68. Ibid., 223.

69. Truman, *Memoirs,* 1:192–193.

70. Evabeth Miller, "Mrs. Truman Is Own Housekeeper," Mary Paxton Keeley Papers, Clipping File, Box 1, HSTL.

71. Quoted in Truman, *Bess W. Truman,* 232.

72. Maurine H. Beasley, "Bess (Elizabeth Virginia Wallace) Truman," *American First Ladies: Their Lives and Their Legacy,* edited by Lewis L. Gould (New York: Garland, 1996), 455.

73. Brian Burnes, "Bess Also Target for Truman Critics," *Kansas City Star,* 27 January 1996, 18. See also Stephen Shadegg, *Clare Booth Luce: A Biography* (New York: Simon & Schuster, 1970), 140.

74. "'No Secret,' Truman Says of Wife's Job in the Senate," *New York Times,* 27 July 1944, 11; "Meet Harry's Boss, Bess," *Collier's,* 12 February 1949, 14.

75. Truman, *Bess W. Truman,* 241–242.

76. Quoted in Robbins, *Bess and Harry,* 71.

77. Ibid., 72–73.

78. Ibid., 74.

79. Bess Truman to Ethel Noland, 30 March 1945, Mary Ethel Noland Papers, Correspondence File, Box 1, HSTL.

80. Truman, *Bess W. Truman,* 249–251.

81. Frances Perkins Oral History Interview, Columbia University Oral History Project, Columbia University.

82. *Eleanor Roosevelt's "My Day": Her Acclaimed Columns, 1936–1945,* Volume 1, ed. Rochele Chadakoff (New York: Pharos Books, 1989), 391.

83. J. B. West, *Upstairs at the White House: My Life with the First Ladies* (New York: Coward, McCann & Geoghegan, 1973), 58.

84. Ibid., 59.

85. Reathal Odum Oral History Interview, HSTL; "Reathel Odum, 97, Trumans' Discreet Secretary," *New York Times,* 24 July 2006, 22.

86. Ibid.

87. Ibid.

88. Ibid.

89. "First Ladies' Aide Is Dead at 88 Here: Trumans to Attend Services," *Washington Daily News,* 7 August 1962, 12.

90. Means, "What Three Presidents Say About Their Wives," 89–90; Gil Troy,

Mr. and Mrs. President: From the Trumans to the Clintons (Lawrence: University Press of Kansas, 2000), 37.

91. Bess Truman to Eleanor Roosevelt, 31 May 1945, Eleanor Roosevelt Papers, Post–White House Correspondence, 1945–1960, Franklin D. Roosevelt Library.

92. Bess Truman to Mary Paxton Keeley, May 12, 1945, Mary Paxton Keeley Papers, Correspondence File, Box 1, HSTL.

93. Truman, *Bess W. Truman,* 225.

CHAPTER 2: BECOMING FIRST LADY

1. "First Lady Swings Bottle Unbroken," *New York Times,* 31 May 1945, 22; Jhan Robbins, *Bess and Harry: An American Love Story* (New York: G. P. Putnam, 1980), 96.

2. Vertical File, Truman Family Files, Bess Wallace Truman—DAR, HSTL. Hazel Scott was not only an accomplished jazz pianist who had trained at the Juilliard School, but also a film actress and the first woman of color to have her own television show. For Hazel Scott, see Karen Chilton, *Hazel Scott: The Pioneering Journey of a Jazz Pianist from Café Society to Hollywood to HUAC* (Ann Arbor: University of Michigan Press, 2008). For Adam Clayton Powell, see Charles V. Hamilton, *Adam Clayton Powell Jr.: The Political Biography of an American Dilemma* (New York: Cooper Square Publishers, 2002).

3. Hamilton, *Adam Clayton Powell Jr.,* 102.

4. For President Truman's reaction, see Gil Troy, *Mr. and Mrs. President: From the Trumans to the Clintons* (Lawrence: University Press of Kansas, 2000), 20.

5. "My Day," 15 October 1945, in *Eleanor Roosevelt's "My Day,"* Volume 2: *First Lady of the World,* edited by David Elmblidge (New York: Pharos Books, 1991), 13; "Bess Truman Attends DAR Tea," *Kansas City Star,* 12 October 1945, 12; "DAR Refuses Auditorium to Hazel Scott: Constitution Hall for White Artists Only," *New York Times,* 11 October 1945, 17.

6. Elsie Alexander to Bess Truman, 13 October 1945, Papers of Harry S. Truman, Records of the White House Social Office, Correspondence File, HSTL.

7. Ethylmae Berg to Bess Truman, 17 October 1945, Papers of Harry S. Truman, Records of the White House Social Office, Correspondence File, HSTL.

8. Bess Truman to Mary Paxton Keeley, 18 October 1945, Mary Paxton Keeley Papers, Correspondence File, Box 1, HSTL.

9. Margaret Truman, *Bess W. Truman* (New York: Macmillan, 1986), 279; "Trumans Condemn D.A.R. Negro Ban," *New York Times,* 13 October 1945, 17.

10. Edith B. Helm Social Functions Scrapbook, Papers of Edith B. Helm, Box 29, Library of Congress.

11. Quotation in Truman, *Bess W. Truman,* 265.

12. Ibid., 266.

13. "The First Lady Is Determined to Avoid the Limelight," *Washington Post,* 14 July 1945, 20, Vertical File, Truman Family File, Bess Wallace Truman—Independence, HSTL.

14. Ibid.

15. Bess Truman to Ethel Noland, 4 September 1945, Mary Ethel Noland Papers, Correspondence File, Box 1, HSTL.

16. Edith Benham Helm, *The Captains and the Kings* (New York: G. P. Putnam's Sons, 1954), 256–258.

17. Bess Furman, "Independent Lady from Independence," Bess Furman Papers, Subject File, Box 54, Library of Congress.

18. "Behind Mrs. Truman's Social Curtain: No Comment," *Newsweek,* 10 November 1947, 16.

19. Quotation in Truman, *Bess W. Truman,* 276–277. For Charlie Ross, see Ronald T. Farrar, *The Reluctant Servant: The Story of Charles G. Ross* (Columbia: University of Missouri Press, 1969).

20. Bess Truman to Mary Paxton Keeley, 12 May 1945, Mary Paxton Keeley Papers, Correspondence File, Box 1, HSTL.

21. "Mrs. Truman's Engagements to Be Given to the Press," 1 February 1949, Papers of Harry S. Truman, Records of the White House Social Office, Social Functions File, HSTL.

22. Mildred Kahler Geare, "Mrs. Truman's First Bow to the Press," *Baltimore News-Post,* 16 May 1945, 22.

23. Marianne Means, "What Three Presidents Say About Their Wives," *Good Housekeeping,* August 1962, 90.

24. Furman, "Independent Lady from Independence."

25. Means, "What Three Presidents Say," 90.

26. Reathel Odum Oral History Interview, Oral History Collection, HSTL.

27. J. B. West, *Upstairs at the White House: My Life with the First Ladies* (New York: Coward, McCann & Geoghegan, 1973), 59.

28. Papers of Alonzo Fields, Subject File—Weekly Menus for White House Employees, HSTL.

29. Means, "What Three Presidents Say," 184.

30. Furman, "Independent Lady from Independence"; West, *Upstairs at the White House,* 73–75.

31. West, *Upstairs at the White House,* 78.

32. Compiled from Papers of Harry S. Truman, Records of the White House Social Office Files, Social Functions Files, Boxes 25–77, HSTL.

33. Quotation in Means, "What Three Presidents Say," 184.

34. "Mrs. Truman's Engagements to Be Given to the Press," 12 April 1949, Papers of Harry S. Truman, Records of the White House Social Office Files, Social Functions File, HSTL.

35. Helm, *The Captains and the Kings*, 270–271.

36. Ibid., 90–91.

37. Ibid., 270–271.

38. Ibid., 92–94.

39. Ibid.; Papers of Alonzo Fields, Subject File—Menus—Official, 1940–1952, Box 2, HSTL.

40. Compiled from Papers of Harry S. Truman, Records of the White House Social Office, Social Functions Files, Boxes 25–77, HSTL.

41. Charley Burke, "Notes on Research into the Truman Clothing Collection at the Truman Library," May 1991, Harry S. Truman Museum, Independence, Missouri. On Madame Agasta, see notes of Katie Louchheim, Papers of Katie Louchheim, Box 8, Library of Congress.

42. "Mrs. Truman's Engagements to Be Given to the Press," 18 June 1945, 14 January 1947, 11 February 1947, 4 April 1949, Papers of Harry S. Truman, Records of the White House Social Office, Social Functions File, Box 25, HSTL.

43. Maurine H. Beasley, "Bess (Elizabeth Virginia Wallace) Truman (1885–1982)" in *American First Ladies*, edited by Lewis L. Gould (New York: Garland, 1996), 459.

44. List compiled from Papers of Harry S. Truman, Records of the White House Social Office, Social Functions File, Boxes 22, 52–62, HSTL.

45. "Veterans," Edith B. Helm Social Functions Scrapbook, Papers of Edith B. Helm, Box 31, Library of Congress.

46. "Bess Wallace Truman Biographical Sketch," Edith B. Helm Social Functions Scrapbook, Papers of Edith B. Helm, Box 1, Library of Congress.

47. Eleanor Roosevelt to Bess Truman, 25 April 1945, Eleanor Roosevelt Papers, Post–White House Correspondence, 1945–1960, Franklin D. Roosevelt Library.

48. Ethel Mockler, *Citizens in Action: The Girl Scout Record, 1912–1947* (New York: Girl Scouts National Organization, 1947), 1–55, 75.

49. Ibid., 56–63. For Lou Henry Hoover's work with the Girl Scouts, see Nancy Beck Young, *Lou Henry Hoover: Activist First Lady* (Lawrence: University Press of Kansas, 2004), 111–139.

50. Mockler, *Citizens in Action,* 63, 96–122.

51. Bess Truman to Mrs. C. Vaughan Ferguson, President of the Girl Scouts, 16 October 1945, Papers of Harry S. Truman, Records of the White House Social Office, Correspondence File, Box 9, HSTL.

52. Mockler, *Citizens in Action,* 125–130.

53. Press Release, 25 May 1948, National Girl Scout News Bureau, Papers of Harry S. Truman, Records of the White House Social Office, Correspondence File, Box 9, HSTL.

54. "Clothes for Friendship Project," 25 May 1948, Papers of Harry S. Truman, Records of the White House Social Office, Correspondence File, Box 9, HSTL.

55. Bess Truman to Mrs. C. Vaughan Ferguson, President of the Girl Scouts, 12 January 1950, Papers of Harry S. Truman, Records of the White House Social Office, Correspondence File, Box 9, HSTL.

56. Bess B. Porter to Bess Truman, 12 February 1950, Papers of Harry S. Truman, Records of the White House Social Office, Correspondence File, Box 9, HSTL.

57. Robbins, *Bess and Harry,* 110–111.

58. "A PEO in the White House," *PEO Record,* June 1945, 23, Vertical File—Bess Truman—PEO, HSTL.

59. Martha P. Caldwell (Chapter S PEO) to Dr. Benedict K. Zoberist, 8 September 1987, Vertical File—Bess Truman—PEO, HSTL.

60. Ibid.

61. "Bess Truman and Her Town," *Life,* 11 July 1946, 89–92, 95–98, 101–102.

62. "No Bridge, This Session Only Conversation for Now Famed Club," *Independence Examiner,* 23 April 1946, 6.

63. Bess Truman, "Do I Miss the White House?," *This Week,* 24 July 1955, 9.

CHAPTER 3: THE WHISTLE-STOP CAMPAIGN AND AFTER

1. Clark Clifford, *Counsel to the President: A Memoir* (New York: Random House, 1991), 190.

2. Gil Troy, *Mr. and Mrs. President: From the Trumans to the Clintons* (Lawrence: University Press of Kansas, 2000), 42.

3. Zachary Karabell, *The Last Campaign: How Harry Truman Won the 1948 Election* (New York: Vintage Books, 2001), 135, 199. For other studies on the 1948 election, see Allen Yarnell, *Democrats and Progressives: The 1948 Presidential Election as a Test of Postwar Liberalism* (Berkeley: University of California Press, 1974); and Richard S. Kirkendall, "Election of 1948," in *History of American Pres-*

idential Elections, edited by Arthur M. Schlesinger Jr. (New York: Chelsea House, 1971).

4. Karabell, *Last Campaign,* 145; Brian Burnes, "Bess Also Target for Truman Critics," *Kansas City Star,* 27 January 1996, 18. President Truman banned Luce from the White House for her comments.

5. Margaret Truman, *Harry S. Truman* (New York: William Morrow, 1973), 4–5.

6. Ibid., 5.

7. Messall quotation in Jhan Robbins, *Bess and Harry: An American Love Story* (New York: G. P. Putnam, 1980), 123.

8. Bray quotation in Robbins, *Bess and Harry,* 123. Earlier first ladies had not campaigned with their husbands, except for Lou Henry Hoover, who did so in 1932. Bess Truman set a precedent for other first ladies who followed her to involve themselves with presidential campaigns.

9. Karabell, *Last Campaign,* 159–160, 191–192. For thorough coverage of Truman and the 80th Congress, see Susan M. Hartmann, *Truman and the 80th Congress* (Columbia: University of Missouri Press, 1971).

10. David McCullough, *Truman* (New York: Simon & Schuster, 1992), 654–655.

11. Ibid., 653.

12. Ibid., 654; Ross quotation in Robbins, *Bess and Harry,* 122.

13. McCullough, *Truman,* 655.

14. Truman, *Harry S. Truman,* 22.

15. Ibid.

16. Ibid., 23.

17. Ibid.

18. Robbins, *Bess and Harry,* 124.

19. Ibid., 123.

20. Ibid., 124; Truman, *Harry S. Truman,* 27–28.

21. Ross quotation in Robbins, *Bess and Harry,* 124.

22. Truman, *Harry S. Truman,* 34; Margaret Truman, *Bess W. Truman* (New York: Macmillan, 1986), 328.

23. Meyer Berger, "Truman on 2d Day Tours for 66 Miles," *New York Times,* 30 October 1948, 1.

24. Truman, *Harry S. Truman,* 38–39; "Truman in St. Louis," *New York Times,* 31 October 1948, 1, 46.

25. Karabell, *Last Campaign,* 251.

26. Truman, *Harry S. Truman,* 39–41.

27. Ibid., 41; Karabell, *Last Campaign,* 254.

28. Margaret Truman, *First Ladies: An Intimate Group Portrait of White House Wives* (New York: Fawcett Books, 1995), 84.

29. Ross quotation in Robbins, *Bess and Harry,* 128.

30. Ibid., 127; Truman, *Harry S. Truman,* 42.

31. Truman, *Bess W. Truman,* 336–338.

32. Ibid.

33. Bess Truman to Mary Paxton Keeley, 4 January 1949, Papers of Mary Paxton Keeley, Correspondence File, Box 1, HSTL.

34. Truman, *Bess W. Truman,* 339.

35. Truman, *Harry S. Truman,* 400; Robbins, *Bess and Harry,* 131.

36. Truman, *Bess W. Truman,* 340.

37. Press Release, 15 January 1949, Papers of Harry S. Truman, Records of the White House Social Office, Social Functions File, HSTL.

38. Truman, *Harry S. Truman,* 402–403.

39. Edith Benham Helm, *The Captains and the Kings* (New York: G. P. Putnam's Sons, 1954), 266–267.

40. Press Release, 15 January 1949, Papers of Harry S. Truman, Records of the White House Social Office, Social Functions File, HSTL.

41. Truman, *Harry S. Truman,* 403; Robbins, *Bess and Harry,* 133.

42. Helen Essary, "The President's Boss, Bess," *Look,* 12 February 1949, 35–37.

43. Jonathan Daniels, "The Lady from Independence," *McCall's,* April 1949, 15.

44. H. Walton Cloke, "Senator Defends First Lady on Gift," *New York Times,* 16 August 1949, 1, 10; Truman, *Bess W. Truman,* 347–348.

45. Bess Truman to Mary Paxton Keeley, 14 April 1949, Papers of Mary Paxton Keeley, Correspondence File, Box. 1, HSTL.

46. Susan M. Hartmann, *The Home Front and Beyond: American Women in the 1940s* (Boston: Twayne, 1982), 148–149. For the public campaigns and private networks of women in politics in the 1950s, see Joanne Meyerowitz, *Not June Cleaver: Women and Gender in Postwar America, 1945–1960* (Philadelphia: Temple University Press, 1994).

47. Edith B. Helm, Social Functions Scrapbook, Teas, Papers of Edith B. Helm, Box 29, Library of Congress; "Mrs. Truman's Engagements to Be Given to the Press," 1 November 1949, 25 April 1950, 31 October 1950, 24 April 1951, 16 October 1951, Papers of Harry S. Truman, Records of the White House Social Office, Social Functions File, HSTL.

48. "Mrs. Truman's Engagements to Be Given to the Press," 14 October 1945,

25 April 1946, 9 May 1946, 5 May 1948, 15 February 1949, 1 November 1949, 31 October 1950, 22 January 1952, Papers of Harry S. Truman, Records of the White House Social Office, Social Functions File, HSTL.

49. Bess Truman to Eleanor Roosevelt, 24 September 1952, Eleanor Roosevelt Papers, Post–White House Correspondence, 1945–1960, Franklin D. Roosevelt Library.

50. Elsie L. George, "The Women Appointees of the Roosevelt and Truman Administrations: A Study of Their Impact and Effectiveness," Ph.D. diss. (The American University, 1972), 88.

51. Ibid., 82–83.

52. Susan Roth Breitzer, "Eleanor Roosevelt: An Unlikely Path to Political Activist," in *The Presidential Companion: Readings on the First Ladies,* edited by Robert P. Watson and Anthony J. Eksterowicz (Columbia: University of South Carolina Press, 2006), 164–165.

53. George, "Women Appointees," 83.

54. Ibid., 84.

55. Ibid., 62. For the opposition to the Equal Rights Amendment, see Hartmann, *The Home Front and Beyond,* 145–146.

56. George, "Women Appointees," 85.

57. Ibid., 65–66.

58. India Edwards, *Pulling No Punches: Memoirs of a Woman in Politics* (New York: G. P. Putnam's Sons, 1977), 111.

59. India Edwards quotation in Robbins, *Bess and Harry,* 87.

60. George, "Women Appointees," 82–86.

61. Edwards, *Pulling No Punches,* 140–141.

62. Eric Pace, "Anna Rosenberg Hoffman Dead: Consultant and 60s Defense Aide," *Washington Post,* 10 May 1983, 14.

63. Ibid.

64. George, "Women Appointees," 89.

65. Harry S. Truman to Perle Mesta, 21 July 1950, Papers of Harry S. Truman, President's Secretary's Files, Box 19, HSTL.

CHAPTER 4: RENOVATING THE WHITE HOUSE

1. William Seale, *The White House: The History of an American Idea* (Washington, D.C.: White House Historical Association, 2001), 233, 235.

2. Ibid.; J. B. West, *Upstairs at the White House: My Life with the First Ladies* (New York: Coward, McCann & Geoghegan, 1973), 97–98.

3. West, *Upstairs at the White House,* 98.

4. Ibid., 98–99.

5. Ibid.

6. Ibid.

7. Seale, *White House,* 238.

8. Ibid.

9. David McCullough, *Truman* (New York: Simon & Schuster, 1992), 877.

10. West, *Upstairs at the White House,* 102.

11. Ibid., 103–104.

12. Ibid., 104.

13. Ibid.

14. Ibid., 104–105.

15. Ibid.

16. Ibid.

17. William Seale, *The President's House: A History* (Washington, D.C.: White House Historical Association, 1986), 1028–1029.

18. Jhan Robbins, *Bess and Harry: An American Love Story* (New York: G. P. Putnam, 1980), 130.

19. Snyder quotation in ibid.

20. Taft quotation in ibid.

21. Winslow quotation in Seale, *White House,* 241.

22. Seale, *President's House,* 659–673.

23. Holly Cowan Shulman, "Dolley Payne Todd Madison," in *American First Ladies: Their Lives and Their Legacy,* 2nd ed., edited by Lewis L. Gould (New York: Routledge, 2001), 27.

24. Betty C. Monkman, *The White House: Its Historic Furnishings and First Families* (Washington, D.C.: White House Historical Association, 2000), 53.

25. Ibid., 93.

26. Ibid., 123: Jean H. Baker, "Mary Ann Todd Lincoln," in Gould, *American First Ladies,* 117–118.

27. Monkman, *White House,* 135, 147, 164.

28. Stacy A. Cordery, "Edith Kermit Carow Roosevelt," in Gould, *American First Ladies,* 205: Seale, *White House,* 167.

29. Monkman, *White House,* 204–208.

30. Ibid, 208–210, 214.

31. McCullough, *Truman,* 878.

32. Ibid.

33. West, *Upstairs at the White House,* 105.

34. Seale, *White House,* 244.

35. McCullough, *Truman,* 879.

36. Ibid.

37. Seale, *White House,* 252.

38. Ibid, 281–281.

39. Ibid.; McCullough, *Truman,* 880.

40. McCullough, *Truman,* 880–881.

41. Ibid.

42. Ibid, 881, 883; Seale, *White House,* 256.

43. Monkman, *White House,* 220–222.

44. *New York Times,* 15 March 1952, 15.

45. McCullough, *Truman,* 884–885.

46. Ibid., 886.

47. Edith Benham Helm, *The Captains and the Kings* (New York: G. P. Putnam's Sons, 1954), 280.

48. Bess Furman, "Redecoration of the White House," Bess Furman Papers, Subject File, Box 54, Library of Congress.

49. Ibid.

50. Ibid.

51. Ibid.

52. White House Press Release, "Interior Decoration of the White House," Vertical File—White House Renovation, HSTL.

53. Ibid.

54. Ibid.

55. Helm, *The Captains and the Kings,* 282.

56. White House Press Release, "Interior Decoration of the White House," Vertical File—White House Renovation, HSTL.

57. Ibid.

58. Ibid.; Helm, *The Captains and the Kings,* 283.

59. Ibid.

60. White House Press Release, "Interior Decoration of the White House," Vertical File—White House Renovation, HSTL.

61. Ibid.

62. Ibid.

63. McCullough, *Truman,* 886.

CHAPTER 5: PARTNER AND ADVISER

1. Marianne Means, "What Three Presidents Say About Their Wives," *Good Housekeeping,* August 1962, 184.

2. Margaret Truman, *First Ladies: An Intimate Group Portrait of White House Wives* (New York: Fawcett Books, 1995), 83.

3. Margaret Truman, *Bess W. Truman* (New York: Macmillan, 1986), 270–274.

4. Truman, *First Ladies,* 84.

5. Ibid., 84–85.

6. Carl Sterrazza Anthony, *First Ladies: The Saga of the Presidents' Wives and Their Power, 1789–1961* (New York: William Morrow), 523.

7. Gil Troy, *Mr. and Mrs. President: From the Trumans to the Clintons* (Lawrence: University Press of Kansas, 2000), 36–27; Harry S. Truman to Bess Truman, 17 July 1945, Papers of Harry S. Truman Pertaining to Family, Business, and Personal Affairs, Box 14, HSTL.

8. J. B. West, *Upstairs at the White House: My Life with the First Ladies* (New York: Coward, McCann & Geoghegan, 1973), 77.

9. Truman, *Bess W. Truman,* 280–281.

10. Harry S. Truman to Bess Truman, 28 December 1945, Papers of Harry S. Truman Pertaining to Family, Business, and Personal Affairs, Box 14, HSTL. This letter is among those collected in *Dear Bess: The Letters from Harry to Bess Truman, 1910–1959,* edited by Robert H. Ferrell (New York: W. W. Norton, 1983), 523–524.

11. Ibid.; Truman, *Bess W. Truman,* 286.

12. James E. St. Clair and Linda C. Gugin, *Chief Justice Fred M. Vinson of Kentucky: A Political Biography* (Lexington: University of Kentucky Press, 2002), 120–125, 190, 192–194.

13. Ibid., 142–157, 166–172, 175–188.

14. Harry S. Truman to Bess Truman, 22 June 1946, Papers of Harry S. Truman Pertaining to Family, Business, and Personal Affairs, Box 15, HSTL.

15. St. Clair and Gugin, *Chief Justice Fred M. Vinson,* 198–201, 219–226, 239–245.

16. Truman, *First Ladies,* 73–75.

17. Ibid.

18. David McCullough, *Truman* (New York: Simon & Schuster, 1992), 513; Margaret Truman, *Harry S. Truman* (New York: William Morrow, 1973), 315–316, Robert H. Ferrell, *Harry S. Truman: A Life* (Columbia: University of Missouri Press, 1994), 224–225.

19. McCullough, *Truman,* 514; Truman, *Harry S. Truman,* 316.

20. McCullough, *Truman,* 515.

21. Ibid., 516; Truman, *Harry S. Truman,* 318; Ferrell, *Harry S. Truman,* 225.

22. Harry S. Truman to Bess Truman, 21 September 1946, Papers of Harry S.

Truman Pertaining to Family, Business, and Personal Affairs, Box 15, HSTL; Ferrell, *Dear Bess,* 539.

23. Truman, *Bess W. Truman,* 344.

24. Ibid.

25. Harry S. Truman to Bess Truman, 14 August 1946, Papers of Harry S. Truman Pertaining to Family, Business, and Personal Affairs, Box 15, HSTL.

26. Irvine H. Anderson, *Aramco, the United States, and Saudi Arabia: A Study of the Dynamics of Foreign Oil Policy, 1933–1950* (Princeton, N.J.: Princeton University Press, 1981), 108–115.

27. Ibid., 115.

28. Ibid., 116–122.

29. Ibid., 123.

30. McCullough, *Truman,* 539–540; Truman, *Harry S. Truman,* 344–345.

31. Ibid.; Ferrell, *Harry S. Truman,* 247.

32. McCullough, *Truman,* 541.

33. Ibid.; Truman, *Harry S. Truman,* 345; Ferrell, *Harry S. Truman,* 251.

34. McCullough, *Truman,* 543–545; Ferrell, *Harry S. Truman,* 248–249.

35. McCullough, *Truman,* 545.

36. Harry S. Truman to Bess Truman, 14 March 1947, Papers of Harry S. Truman Pertaining to Family, Business, and Personal Affairs, Box 16, HSTL.

37. McCullough, *Truman,* 553–554.

38. Ibid., 561–562; Truman, *Harry S. Truman,* 352.

39. McCullough, *Truman,* 563; Truman, *Harry S. Truman,* 353; Ferrell, *Harry S. Truman,* 255.

40. McCullough, *Truman,* 564; Truman, *Harry S. Truman,* 353.

41. Harry S. Truman to Bess Truman, 30 September 1947, Papers of Harry S. Truman Pertaining to Family, Business, and Personal Affairs, Box 16, HSTL.

42. McCullough, *Truman,* 565–566; Truman, *Harry S. Truman,* 354–356.

43. Truman, *Harry S. Truman,* 357; Ferrell, *Harry S. Truman,* 256.

44. Truman, *Bess W. Truman,* 355–356.

45. Harry S. Truman, *Memoirs of Harry S. Truman, 1946–1952:* Volume 2, *Years of Trial and Hope* (Garden City, N.Y.: Doubleday, 1956), 332.

46. Harry S. Truman to Bess Truman, 26 June 1950, Papers of Harry S. Truman Pertaining to Family, Business, and Personal Affairs, Box 16, HSTL; Ferrell, *Dear Bess,* 562.

47. Dean Acheson, *Present at the Creation: My Years in the State Department* (New York: Penguin, 1969), 411–413.

48. McCullough, *Truman,* 770.

49. Ibid.; Truman, *Harry S. Truman,* 526–527.

50. Truman, *Harry S. Truman,* 527.

51. Ibid., 530–532; McCullough, *Truman,* 887–891.

52. McCullough, *Truman,* 892; Truman, *Harry S. Truman,* 532.

53. Truman, *Bess W. Truman,* 380–381.

54. Ibid., 381–382.

55. Ibid., 382–383; McCullough, *Truman,* 892–893.

56. Rayburn quotation in Jhan Robbins, *Bess and Harry: An American Love Story* (New York: G. P. Putnam, 1980), 152.

57. Snyder quotation in ibid., 152–153.

CHAPTER 6: RETIREMENT

1. Margaret Truman, *Bess W. Truman* (New York: Macmillan, 1986), 394.

2. Margaret Truman, *Harry S. Truman* (New York: William Morrow, 1973), 558–559.

3. Truman, *Bess W. Truman,* 396.

4. Ibid.; Jhan Robbins, *Bess and Harry: An American Love Story* (New York: G. P. Putnam, 1980), 155–156.

5. Truman, *Bess W. Truman,* 393.

6. David McCullough, *Truman* (New York: Simon & Schuster, 1992), 928.

7. Snyder quotation in Robbins, *Bess and Harry,* 156.

8. McCullough, *Truman,* 929.

9. Bess Truman, "Do I Miss the White House?," *This Week,* 24 July 1955, 8–9.

10. Truman, *Bess W. Truman,* 400.

11. Ibid.

12. Bess Truman to Mary Paxton Keeley, 18 March 1953, Mary Paxton Keeley Papers, Correspondence File, Box 1, HSTL.

13. Truman, *Bess W. Truman,* 400–401.

14. Harry S. Truman, *Mr. Citizen* (New York: Geis, 1960), 64.

15. Ibid., 65.

16. Ibid, 65–66; McCullough, *Truman,* 933–934.

17. Margaret Truman, *Souvenir: Margaret Truman's Own Story* (New York: McGraw-Hill, 1956), 342.

18. Truman, *Bess W. Truman,* 397.

19. Ibid.

20. Transcript from *Person to Person,* 25 May 1955, in Truman, *Souvenir,* 342.

21. Truman, *Harry S. Truman,* 564.

22. McCullough, *Truman,* 936–938, 941.

23. Truman, *Bess W. Truman,* 411.

24. Harry S. Truman, *Memoirs:* Volume 1, *Year of Decisions* (New York: Doubleday), iii.

25. Truman, *Bess W. Truman,* 411; Harry S. Truman to John W. McCormack, 10 January 1957, in *Off the Record: The Private Papers of Harry S. Truman,* edited by Robert H. Ferrell (New York: Harper and Row, 1980), 346–347.

26. Truman, *Bess W. Truman,* 411–412.

27. Ibid., 403.

28. McCullough, *Truman,* 943.

29. Ibid., 946: Truman, *Bess W. Truman,* 403–404.

30. Truman, *Bess W. Truman,* 406.

31. Ibid., 407; Margaret Hamilton, "Margaret Is a Radiant Bride," *Kansas City Star,* 22 April 1956, 1.

32. Truman, *Bess W. Truman,* 407.

33. "'Ordinary Citizen' Still Truman Goal," *Kansas City Star,* 10 April 1956, 1–2; McCullough, *Truman,* 952–959.

34. Ibid.

35. Tom Evans Oral History Interview, HSTL; Truman, *Bess W. Truman,* 404–405; McCullough, *Truman,* 959–960.

36. Truman, *Bess W. Truman,* 408; photograph of Mr. and Mrs. Truman at hospital, *New York Times,* 7 June 1957, 3; Bess Truman to Mary Paxton Keeley, 1 February 1958, Mary Paxton Keeley Papers, Correspondence File, Box 1, HSTL.

37. McCullough, *Truman,* 966–967.

38. Marianne Means, "What Three Presidents Say About Their Wives," *Good Housekeeping,* August 1962, 191; Bess Truman to Mary Paxton Keeley, 2 February 1960, Mary Paxton Keeley Papers, Correspondence File, Box 1, HSTL.

39. Bess Truman to Katie Louchheim, 24 June 1958, Papers of Katie Louchheim, Box 4, Library of Congress.

40. Bess Truman to Katie Louchheim, 14 May 1959, Papers of Katie Louchheim, Box 4, Library of Congress.

41. Truman, *Bess W. Truman,* 412–413.

42. Ibid., 419; Means, "What Three Presidents Say," 192.

43. Truman, *Harry S. Truman,* 579.

44. Truman, *Bess W. Truman,* 414–416; McCullough, *Truman,* 970–974.

45. Papers of John F. Kennedy, President's Office Files, Box 10, John F. Kennedy Library.

46. Papers of John F. Kennedy, White House Social Files, Box 35, John F. Kennedy Library; Truman, *Bess W. Truman*, 481; Truman, *Harry S. Truman*, 573–574.

47. Truman, *Bess W. Truman*, 418.

48. Ibid., 419; McCullough, *Truman*, 983–984.

49. Truman, *Bess W. Truman*, 419.

50. McCullough, *Truman*, 986.

51. Ibid., 987–988; Truman, *Bess W. Truman*, 421.

52. Truman, *Bess W. Truman*, 422.

53. Ibid.; McCullough, *Truman*, 988–989.

54. Truman, *Bess W. Truman*, 424–426.

55. Ibid., 426–428.

56. Ibid., 427.

57. Ibid., 411, 417, 431.

58. Ibid., 431; "Bess Truman, 97, Dies at Home," *Kansas City Star*, 19 October 1982, 1.

59. Truman, *Bess W. Truman*, 432.

60. Ronald Reagan and Jimmy Carter quotations in "Bess Truman, 97, Dies at Home"; "Remembering Bess," *Washington Post*, 19 October 1982, D1.

BIBLIOGRAPHIC ESSAY

This book draws primarily from the Papers of Harry S. Truman and from the manuscript collections of Bess Truman's contemporaries at the Harry S. Truman Library and the Library of Congress. The Papers of Harry S. Truman are subdivided into the Records of the White House Social Office and the Papers Pertaining to Family, Business, and Personal Affairs.

The twenty-five linear feet of records of the White House Social Office illuminate Mrs. Truman's busy White House social schedule and detail the efforts of one of the busiest White House hostesses. "Mrs. Truman's Engagements to Be Given to the Press" are located in this collection. Included are five linear feet of Office of Social Correspondence files that contain hundreds of pieces of correspondence that Bess Truman received, as well as her correspondence to organizations.

The 12.8 linear feet of President Truman's Papers Pertaining to Family, Business, and Personal Affairs include handwritten letters, legal documents, financial records, newspaper clippings, and other printed material. More than half of this collection is composed of the 1,600 surviving letters from Harry to Bess. Boxes 14 through 16 hold the letters the president wrote to the first lady. These boxes should be consulted for evidence about the manner in which Harry and Bess Truman communicated during his presidency and worked with each other.

Several collateral collections at the Truman Library were consulted for this book. Most important are the Mary Paxton Keeley Papers. Keeley was a lifelong friend of Bess Truman from Independence. Box 1 contains letters Bess wrote Mary and a newspaper clipping file on Mrs. Truman. There are four linear feet of the Reathel Odum Papers. This comprises primarily scrapbooks and Miss Odum's appointment books; Odum was personal secretary to Truman. Boxes 5 and 6 contain a few letters that Bess wrote to Odum. Three linear feet of the Mary Ethel Noland Papers contain one box of letters Bess wrote to the Noland family (Mary was Harry S. Truman's cousin). The David F. Wallace Papers comprise approximately sixty pages of documents, consisting primarily of correspondence from Bess and Harry to Wallace, Bess Truman's nephew. A few letters are addressed to Fred Wallace (Bess's youngest brother) and to David F.

Wallace's mother, Christine. The Alonzo Fields Papers contain menus that Fields prepared for state dinners as well as Truman family meals. Mrs. Truman has made margin suggestions on many of the menus. Fields was chief butler in the White House from 1933 to 1953.

The Truman Library Oral History Collection contains many valuable records, including those of Clark M. Clifford, India Edwards, Tom Evans, Dr. Wallace H. Graham, Mary Paxton Keeley, Charles Murphy, Mary Ethel Noland, Reathel Odum, Mize Peters, and Katie Louchheim.

Three collections in the Library of Congress Manuscript Division also informed this book: the Papers of Edith Benham Helm (social secretary at the White House from 1919 to 1953), Bess Furman (reporter for the *New York Times*), and Katie Louchheim (vice chair of the Democratic National Committee from 1956 to 1960).

The Papers of Edith Benham Helm are subdivided into Social Functions Scrapbooks, Press Briefing Material, and White House Scrapbooks. Boxes 29 through 31 of the Social Functions Scrapbooks shed light on Bess Truman's social engagements. "Mrs. Truman's Engagements to Be Given to the Press" are also found in the Press Briefing Material. White House and other invitations primarily make up the White House Scrapbooks. The Papers of Bess Furman are subdivided into General Correspondence and Subject File. Only one thank-you note from Mrs. Truman is located in General Correspondence. The Subject File on Bess Truman contains six folders of Furman's notes and articles written on the first lady. The Papers of Katie Louchheim contain letters Mrs. Truman wrote to Louchheim, which informed this book on the postpresidential years.

The popular press published many articles about Bess Truman during her adult life, making magazine and newspaper sources extremely useful. Researchers interested in Bess's public voice should see Bess Truman, "Do I Miss the White House?," *This Week* magazine (Washington), 24 July 1955, 7–9. An important glimpse into her relationship with Harry S. Truman can be found in Edith Asbury, "The President's Boss . . . Bess Truman," *Look,* 1 March 1949, 3–9, and Helen Essary, "The President's Boss, Bess," *Look,* 12 February 1949, 2–7. Jonathan Daniels reveals Truman's background in Independence in "The Lady from Independence," *McCall's,* April 1949, 10–14. For Truman's first ladyship, see Bess Furman, "Independent Lady from Independence," *New York Times,* 12 July 1946, 20–21, and Doris Fleeson, "Washington's Ten Most Powerful Women," *McCall's,* January 1951, 5–8. For glimpses into Bess's retirement years, see Margaret Cousins, "A Valentine for Bess Truman," *McCall's,* February 1975. Particularly revealing is Marianne Means, "What Three Presidents Say About Their Wives,"

Good Housekeeping, August 1963, 184–186, 190–193. For an in-depth portrait, see Gerry Van der Heuvel, "Remembering Bess: Farewell to the First Lady Who Shunned 'This Awful Public Life,'" *Washington Post,* 19 October 1982, D1, D3.

There are several memoirs from the period of Bess Truman's first ladyship. Three useful books detail the experiences of some White House staffers during the Truman era: Edith Benham Helm, *The Captains and the Kings* (New York: G. P. Putnam's Sons, 1954); J. B. West, *Upstairs at the White House: My Life with the First Ladies* (New York: Coward, McCann & Geoghegan, 1973); and Lillian Rogers, *My Thirty Years Backstairs at the White House* (New York: Fleet, 1961). For a journalistic account of the early Truman years, see Bess Furman, *Washington By-line: The Personal History of a Newspaperwoman* (New York: Alfred A. Knopf, 1949). Memoirs of those on the inside of the Truman White House include Clark Clifford, *Counsel to the President: A Memoir* (New York: Random House, 1991), and Dean Acheson, *Present at the Creation: My Years in the State Department* (New York: Penguin, 1969). For the appointment of women to the Truman administration and operations of the Democratic National Committee, see India Edwards, *Pulling No Punches: Memoirs of a Woman in Politics* (New York: G. P. Putnam, 1977). For Margaret Truman's life in the White House and after, including her relationship with her parents, see Margaret Truman, *Souvenir: Margaret Truman's Own Story* (New York: McGraw-Hill, 1956).

President Truman's own memoir, *Memoirs of Harry S. Truman, 1945:* Volume 1, *Year of Decisions* (Garden City, N.Y.: Doubleday, 1955), and *Memoirs of Harry S. Truman, 1946–1952:* Volume 2, *Years of Trial and Hope* (Garden City, N.Y.: Doubleday, 1956), gives details of the close relationship between the president and the first lady but provides little insight into her influence on his decisions. Harry S. Truman, *Mr. Citizen* (New York: Geis, 1960), provides wonderful insights into the Trumans' lives during the early postpresidential years.

The official biography of Bess Truman is Margaret Truman's valuable study of her mother, which portrays Mrs. Truman as a reluctant politician's wife and as a feisty no-nonsense first lady whose considerable influence on her husband remained largely hidden from public view. Researchers must consult Margaret Truman, *Bess W. Truman* (New York: Macmillan, 1986). Two other insightful but shorter biographies are Maurine H. Beasley, "Bess (Elizabeth Virginia Wallace) Truman," in *First Ladies: Their Lives and Their Legacy,* edited by Lewis L. Gould (New York: Routledge, 2001), and Margot Ford McMillen and Heather Roberson, "Bess Wallace Truman," in *Into the Spotlight: Four Missouri Women* (Columbia: University of Missouri Press, 2004). On Mrs. Truman's private life and private influence, see Raymond Frey, "Bess W. Truman: The Reluctant First

Lady," in *The Presidential Companion: Readings on the First Ladies,* edited by Robert Watson and Anthony J. Eksterowicz (Columbia: University of South Carolina Press, 2006). On the Trumans, privacy, and gentility, see Gil Troy, "Just the Wife of the President," in *Mr. and Mrs. President: From the Trumans to the Clintons* (Lawrence: University Press of Kansas, 2000). Researchers interested in the Trumans' courtship and marriage should also consult Jhan Robbins, *Bess and Harry: An American Love Story* (New York: G. P. Putnam, 1980).

Several secondary source accounts of first ladies and of women's history provided a comparative and theoretical basis for this book. The most important were Carl Sferrazza Anthony, *First Ladies: The Saga of the President' Wives and Their Power, 1789–1961* (New York: William Morrow, 1990); Betty Boyd Caroli, *First Ladies,* expanded edition (New York: Oxford University Press, 1995); and Myra G. Gutin, *The President's Partner: The First Lady in the Twentieth Century* (Westport, Conn.: Greenwood Press, 1991). A collection edited by Sara Alpern, Joyce Antler, Elisabeth Israels Perry, and Ingrid Winther Scobie, *The Challenge of Feminist Biography: Writing the Lives of Modern American Women* (Urbana: University of Illinois Press, 1992), covers the issues involved in writing feminist biography. Historical interest in first ladies has increased in recent years, thanks in large part to Lewis Gould, a leading presidential historian and editor of the series this book is a part of, who authored "First Ladies," *American Scholar* 55 (1986): 528–535, and "Modern First Ladies in Historical Perspective," *Presidential Studies Quarterly* 15 (1985): 537, while editing the encyclopedic *American First Ladies: Their Lives and Their Legacies* (New York: Routledge, 2001).

Many volumes on Harry S. Truman's life and presidency provide the context in which Bess Truman's life developed. The definitive account is David McCullough, *Truman* (New York: Simon & Schuster, 1992). McCullough credits Bess Truman with being the most important person in Harry S. Truman's life. The other Truman biographers do not reflect a consensus about Mrs. Truman's role; see Jonathan Daniels, *The Man of Independence* (Philadelphia: Lippincott, 1950); Robert J. Donovan, *Conflict and Crises: The Presidency of Harry S. Truman, 1945–1948* (New York: W. W. Norton, 1977); *Tumultuous Years: The Presidency of Harry S. Truman, 1949–1953* (New York: W. W. Norton, 1982); Donald R. McCoy, *The Presidency of Harry S. Truman* (Lawrence: University Press of Kansas, 1984); Robert H. Ferrell, *Harry Truman: A Life* (Columbia: University of Missouri Press, 1994); and Alonzo Hamby, *Man of the People: A Life of Harry S. Truman* (New York: Oxford University Press, 1995). Margaret Truman's official biography of her father explains the Truman partnership and provides some insights into Bess Truman's role in the 1948 whistle-stop campaign. Researchers should consult Margaret Truman, *Harry S. Truman* (New York: William Morrow, 1973).

Works about the public activities of mid-twentieth-century women also proved useful. Nancy F. Cott, William L. O'Neill, and Rosalind Rosenberg each provide important treatments of feminism. See Cott, *The Grounding of Modern Feminism* (New Haven, Conn.: Yale University Press, 1987); O'Neill, *Everyone Was Brave: A History of Feminism in America* (Chicago: Quadrangle Books, 1971); and Rosenberg, *Beyond Separate Spheres: Intellectual Roots of Modern Feminism* (New Haven, Conn.: Yale University Press, 1982). An analysis of the relationship between women's voluntary associations and reform can be found in Anne Firor Scott, *Making the Invisible Woman Visible* (Urbana: University of Illinois Press, 1984). Robyn Muncy, Lois Scharf and Joan M. Jensen, and Susan Hartmann provide more general discussions of women's activism. See Muncy, *Creating a Female Dominion in American Reform, 1890–1935* (New York: Oxford University Press, 1991); Scharf and Jensen, *Decades of Discontent: The Women's Movement, 1920–1940* (Boston: Northeastern University Press, 1987); and Hartmann, *The Home Front and Beyond: American Women in the 1940s* (Boston: Twayne, 1982). Glenna Matthews constructed an account of how women emerged into the public sphere. See Matthews, *The Rise of Public Woman: Woman's Power and Woman's Place in the United States, 1630–1970* (New York: Oxford University Press, 1992). For the public campaigns and private networks of women in politics in the 1950s, see Joanne Meyerowitz, *Not June Cleaver: Women and Gender in Postwar America, 1945–1960* (Philadelphia, Pa.: Temple University Press, 1994).

Several other secondary sources provided helpful background on specific aspects of Bess Truman's first ladyship. For more information on the 1948 election, see Zachary Karabell, *The Last Campaign: How Harry Truman Won the 1948 Election* (New York: Vintage Books, 2000); Allen Yarnell, *Democrats and Progressives: The 1948 Presidential Election as a Test of Postwar Liberalism* (Berkeley: University of California Press, 1974); and Richard S. Kirkendall, "Election of 1948," in *History of American Presidential Elections,* edited by Arthur M. Schlesinger Jr. (New York: Chelsea House, 1971). For the nomination of Chief Justice Fred M. Vinson and the Vinson Court, see James E. St. Clair and Linda C. Gugin, *Chief Justice Fred M. Vinson of Kentucky: A Political Biography* (Lexington: University Press of Kentucky, 2002). For the resignation of Henry A. Wallace, see Norman D. Markowitz, *The Rise and Fall of the People's Century: Henry A. Wallace and American Liberalism, 1941–1948* (New York: Free Press, 1973). For the crisis over Greece and Turkey and the Truman Doctrine, see John

Lewis Gaddis, "Was the Truman Doctrine a Real Turning Point?" *Foreign Affairs* 52 (1973–1974): 386–402. For the Marshall Plan, see Michael J. Hogan, *The Marshall Plan: America, Britain, and the Reconstruction of Western Europe, 1947–1952* (New York: Cambridge University Press, 1987). For the Korean War, see Burton I. Kaufman, *The Korean War: Challenges in Crisis, Credibility, and Command* (Philadelphia: Pa.: Temple University Press, 1986).

Finally, for researchers interested in Bess Truman's own recipes, including her famous Ozark pudding, see *The Bess Collection: Recipes and Remembrances* (Independence, Mo.: Independence Junior Service League, 1993).

INDEX